PRINCETON THEOLOGICAL MONOGRAPH SERIES

Dikran Y. Hadidian

General Editor

16

A GENTLEMAN IN EVERY SLUM

Church of England Missions in East London
1873-1914

A Gentleman In Every Slum

Church of England Missions in East London

1837-1914

By

David B. McIlhiney

PICKWICK PUBLICATIONS

ALLISON PARK, PENNSYLVANIA

Published by Pickwick Publications
4137 Timberlane Drive, Allison Park, PA 15101-2932

Library of Congress Cataloging-in-Publication Data

McIlhiney, David Brown, 1942-
    A gentleman in every slum : Church of England missions in east London.
1837-1914 / by David B. McIlhiney.
        p.   cm. -- (Princeton theological monograph series : 16)
    Bibliography : p.
    ISBN 0-915138-95-6
    1. Church of England--Missions--England--London. 2. Anglican   Commun
ion--Missions--England--London. 3. City missions--England--London. 4.
Slums--England--London. 5. Evangelicalism--Church of England. 6. London
(England)--Church history. I. Title. II. Series.
BV2865.M38 1988
266'.34215--dc19   88-39913
                                                              C I P

For M.

CONTENTS

PREFACE

Perhaps all attempts to write history are at least modestly revisionist. This work is no exception, for in studying the Church of England in the Victorian era, I have been struck by what seemed two major failings. First, since the most conspicuous movements of the period emanated from the high church party, the creativeness of the evangelicals and the broad churchmen has consistently been undervalued. And second, since church history is largely written by academicians, theological controversies have been treated extensively at the expense of the parish life of the time. What is missing from so much English church history is any sense of the church as most ordinary Christians knew it, the day-by-day life in their local parishes. This work attempts to correct these failings within a very limited area, the slums of East London.

I chose this area because the East End exercised a peculiar fascination for churchmen of Victorian and Edwardian times. From Wapping to Bethnal Green, from Aldgate to the East India Docks, this blighted home of nearly one million people embodied, as did no other district, the new fact of the urban slum. Contemporaries saw the church's mission to the East End as a crucial test of the Establishment, if not of Christianity itself. Largely as a result, the East End diverted hundreds of young clergymen and women church workers from service in the foreign mission field; later historians have pointed to their labors as a high-water mark for the Victorian church. Charles Lowder, particularly, has often been cited as the symbol of saintly dedication to the poor. Yet little is known of Lowder apart from one hagiographical biography, and even that volume is almost unobtainable in the United States. Lowder's colleagues in East London, some of whom were prominent exponents of other theological positions, are largely unremembered today. In their own time, however, the future of the Christian church in Britain was often believed to stand or fall on the success or failure of their ministries.

My debts to individuals are manifold. Prof. Horton Davies of

Princeton University was much more than an academic mentor; he has become my advocate, confidant, and friend. The late Canon Cheslyn Jones, former Principal of Pusey House, was my constantly encouraging gadfly. Father Michael Foizey, then Rector of St. Peter's, London Docks, took me in as his "honorary curate" and fed me with far more than his culinary talents. The late Mrs. Dorothy Mary Gowing, daughter of the first Bishop of Chelmsford, graciously shared with me her early memories of Bethnal Green. My fellow-countrywoman Dr. Lida Elizabeth Ellsworth, who was already embarked on her study of Lowder and the ritualist movement, generously shared with me her material and her discoveries.

My institutional indebtedness is just as considerable. To the librarians and archivists of the Bodleian Library and Pusey House in Oxford, the British Museum and Sion College in London, the Greater London Record Office, Firestone and Speer Libraries in Princeton, and the Library of Congress I owe much. The Episcopal Church Foundation supported my research, and the Protestant Episcopal Theological Seminary in Virginia welcomed me in order that I might write the original version of this study.

I cannot close without a very special acknowledgment. By any standard the reading of parish records is less than exciting. For six months the owners and patrons of the public house of the White Swan in Wapping helped keep me sane. Valiantly they attempted to aid my research, ransacking both their closets and their memories for material that might help. To them I owe a special debt of friendship.

I

THE EAST LONDON SLUMS

At no time in its history was East London simply one unrelieved slum. Beginning as a Roman parade ground in the first century, the three square miles just beyond Aldgate and Bishopsgate can even claim a proud past. To this day their main artery (Whitechapel Road) follows the route of the old Roman highway. In medieval times the village of Stepney grew up there, and in the tenth century the parish church of All Saints was erected a mile and a half from the City walls. Rebuilt two centuries later as St. Dunstan's, the church still stands, one of London's oldest and loveliest structures. When the Palace of Westminster burned in the thirteenth century, King Edward I summoned Parliament to meet in a house located on Stepney Green. A hundred years later Chaucer lived directly over Aldgate and is said to have composed several of his works while looking out across the Stepney fields. It was still a pleasant prospect in the sixteenth century, when Thomas More wrote the Vicar of St. Dunstan's, John Colet, thanking him for a visit: "Wheresoever you look, the earth yieldeth you a pleasant prospect; the temperature of the air fresheth you, and the very bounds of heaven do delight you. Here you find nothing but bounteous gifts of nature and saint-like tokens of innocency."[2] But the next century brought a series of changes that permanently altered this bucolic aspect.

Foremost among these changes was immigration. First, Cromwell re-admitted Jews to the country after a banishment of more than three hundred years. Several thousand arrived in the generation following the Civil War, many settling in Whitechapel and Mile End, not far from the wharves at which their ships had docked. Today one can still see the seventeenth and eighteenth century Sephardic cemetery just off the old Roman road. Second, a wave of French Huguenots arrived after the revocation of the Edict of Nantes. Some were prosperous silk-weavers, and they established a colony in Spitalfields, following their trade until it collapsed in the Victorian era. Third, Irishmen began to arrive at the same period, settling along the Thames and gradually assuming an ever-larger share of the laborers' Posts at the wharves. East London, essentially a rural village until the early seventeenth century, had begun the process of urbanization.

Perhaps the most striking single feature of East London's history is the speed of its transformation between 1700 and 1800. At the beginning of the century the area's population was perhaps 75,000, a figure that would multiply in the next hundred years. Some of the immigrants were skilled tradesmen who settled only briefly in Stepney. But many more were destitute and unskilled, lacking any prospects for rising socially. They tended to cluster near the river--in Wapping, Shadwell, Ratcliff, and St. George's-in-the-East--gradually transforming already populous districts into crowded slums. Writing in the middle of the nineteenth century, Henry Mayhew attributed the worst of the "rookeries" to this rapid growth a hundred and fifty years before.[2] The future direction of all this expansion was not evident in 1720, when a second-generation East Londoner, the distinguished annalist John Strype, wrote of his home:

> Stepney may be esteemed rather a Province than a Parish, especially if we add that it contains in it both City and Country. For towards the South Parts, where it lies along the River Thames for a great way, by Limehouse, Poplar and Ratcliffe, to Wapping, it is furnished with everything that may entitle it to the Honour (if not of a City, yet) of a Great Town; Populousness, Traffick, Commerce, Havens, Shipping, Manufacture, Plenty of wealth, the Crown of All. And were it not eclipsed by the Lustre of the neighbouring City, it would appear one of the Considerable Towns of the Kingdom, and would give place to very few Cities in England. [3]

The wealth, however, increasingly fled to the west. The later years of the eighteenth century were marked by the rapid construction, unregulated by any sanitary legislation, of shoddy tenements and extensions to already decaying houses. "These golden years for jerry-builders and owners of town property....There was no planning, and no authority to insist on any standard." [4] Inevitably, the increasing population pushed the slums northward, away from the Thames. In 1777, when John Wesley visited a group of Methodists in East London, he recorded in his Journal: "I began visiting those of our society who lived in Bethnal Green Hamlet. Many of them I found in such poverty as few can conceive without seeing it." [5] With occasional exceptions, such as part of Spitalfields, the area around St. Dunstan's, and the easternmost reaches of Bethnal Green, East London had very largely evolved into a single slum in the space of only one century. Already its economy had become dominated by the wharves, where many of its male residents found at least casual employment. Already it had gained a reputation for both prostitution and child-abandonment. And already it had become the center for London's criminal element. In 1797 the City's merchants figured that they were losing 10,000 pounds every week to the East London thieves who preyed on their shipping. [6] East London had been transformed from the pleasant village of Stepney into the "East End" that Charles Dickens would make famous.

The Economics of a Slum[7]

Despite his best efforts, H. J. Dyos has been unable to give an explicit meaning to the word "slum": "It is not possible now to invent a satisfactory definition of a slum, even a London one, in the nineteenth century." [8] But if the East London slums defy definition, their origins are nonetheless clear. These blighted areas resulted from two fundamental shortages: those of housing and employment. Until recently it was widely believed that immigration continued to be an important factor, but Dyos has now shown that provincial migrants tended to settle in London's outer perimeter. The so-called "inner circle" of East London, which grew to include more than half a million residents by the end of Victoria's reign, consisted largely of people born in the area. East London encompassed a settled and rapidly reproducing population of slum-dwellers whose condition, with few exceptions, steadily worsened throughout the nineteenth century.

The housing crisis had one obvious cause: a growing population inhabiting a fixed number of buildings. Several factors prevented any increase in the number of housing units: the lack of undeveloped land, the complexity of British land laws, and the attraction of capital away from the inner metropolitan area to the newly developing "suburbs", where the rate of return on investment was substantially higher. Few noncommercial buildings were constructed in East London between 1830 and the end of the century. Indeed, the number of available housing units actually fell steadily throughout the Victorian era as slums were cleared to make room for business expansion, displacing large numbers of people without providing any substitute accommodations.

The first offenders were the docks. Until their construction, all ocean-going ships had been moored in the middle of the Thames and unloaded into the flat-bottomed "lighters" that carried their cargoes to the wharves. The archaic system, necessitated by the river's tidal fluctuations, permitted an incredible degree of pilfering. Probably the lighterman's best-known ploy was simply to throw large amounts of cargo overboard near the riverbank, where it could be retrieved the following night at low tide. The construction of the six East London dock systems between 1800 and 1869 was an effort to end such thievery. Each dock was built around a large inland reservoir kept at high-water level by a series of locks. Each was surrounded by a towering wall and patrolled by private guards who searched the dockworkers before they left the company's premises. The effort was successful. Pilfering practically came to an end, but the human cost was great. [9] The construction of the London Docks between 1800 and 1805 destroyed 1300 houses, displacing probably ten times as many people. Nearly 50,000 residents must have lost their houses to the six dock systems, and perhaps nearly an equal number were dislodged to make room for the many warehouses that increasingly sprang up around the docks. These people had no option but to move north into the already overcrowded areas of Whitechapel, Mile End, Bethnal Green, and Stepney.

The second offenders were the railways. In the twelve short years between 1839 and 1851, three major railway lines were constructed through East London leading to stations just inside the City. While no accurate displacement figures have survived, they seem to have been only somewhat less destructive than the docks. Their effect was most acute in Whitechapel and Bethnal Green, which at the same time were having to accommodate refugees from the riverside.

The third, and in many ways the most reprehensible, offender was the Metropolitan Board of Works. Beginning about 1840, the Board supported the construction of new streets and the widening of others throughout London. The two-mile long Commercial Road, the broadest artery in East London, was cut straight through hundreds of tenements in order to provide an easy access to the East and West India Docks. But many of the Board's projects lacked such a clear rationale. By the middle of the century, "street clearance was imbued with an almost magical efficacy." [10] Certainly the new roads were deliberately planned to break up the worst of the slum areas. Such destruction of the poorest housing, it was thought, together with the increased mobility the new streets made possible, would promote the dispersion of the poor throughout the greater metropolitan area. That such dispersion never took place hardly deterred the Board. Shoreditch and Bethnal Green, especially, were given almost entirely new grids of streets. Dyos quotes one determined supporter of the policy: "Let a good, broad, straight thoroughfare be cut through it from North to South: the whole district is at once opened up and plenty of elbow room given to the city." [11] But all the policy did was to ensure even greater crowding in the areas that had already become slums.

There is a presumably apocryphal story that is often repeated in the contemporary literature on nineteenth century East London. It concerns a room in which five families lived, four occupying the corners and one the middle of that small space. All were said to get on quite well together until the family in the middle took in a lodger. The story was an exaggeration, but the situation it caricatured was nonetheless real. An 1887 study showed that in St. George's in-the-East, almost half the working-men and their families occupied single rooms or less. [12] In extreme cases two and even three families did share the same quarters. And it was common practice for two families, one of whom worked by day and the other by night, to rent the same room; it proved economically more efficient to have the beds occupied around the clock. Such overcrowding certainly owed much to East London's declining economy throughout the Victorian period, but it was magnified by the demolitions for dock, railway, and street construction. Jones has provided figures which, when analyzed, reveal the effect of these demolitions. Eight of the poorest areas within Shoreditch, Bethnal Green, and Whitechapel provided an average of 29.52 houses per acre in 1841. By 1881 the same areas averaged only 23.47 houses per acre. [13] Charles Booth's later statistics reveal that the housing situation only worsened between 1881 and 1901.

Dyos has argued that a lack of housing was the major determinant of any Victorian slum, and it is hard to fault his judgment. But Jones has shown that an equally important factor, at least for East London, was an economy based on "casual" labor. The casual nature of most dock work has long been recognized. Jones' contribution has been to prove that intermittent employment was typical of almost every industry in the metropolitan area. The key point is that London, unlike the cities of the Midlands and the north, never developed a factory system. Jones estimates that as late as the eighteen-nineties, no more than one-sixth of the adult labor force was employed in factories. [14] Rather, London's industry, apart from the construction trades, was concentrated on the finishing crafts, such as the manufacture of clothing, furniture, and precision tools. These were all labor-intensive, generating no great numbers of jobs for semi-skilled workers. London's industry was therefore concentrated in the hands of small masters, the majority of whom had fewer than five employees until the close of the Victorian era. Jones notes Mayhew's observation that a cabinetmaker needed only to marry a servant girl who had saved three or four pounds in order to set himself up as an employer. The result was that London's industry lacked both the capital and the administrative capacity to expand with the city's increasing population. More and more East Londoners became marginal to the work force as the century progressed.

At the beginning of Victoria's reign there were three staple industries in East London: silk-weaving, ship-building, and the docks. By the end of her reign, the first two had collapsed and the third was in a serious decline. Silk manufacturing had practically disappeared by the end of the century. Similarly, in just the six years between 1865 and 1871, employment in ship-building fell by seventy-five percent. [15] To make East London's unemployment even worse, activity at the docks began to fall shortly after 1850. There were several causes. The construction of both new wharves and more efficient dock systems further downstream, for example, increasingly cut into the volume of cargo unloaded at the older docks systems. But the most important factor was the introduction of steamships, which gradually overtook the sailing vessels after 1870. Because the old docks were not large enough to accommodate the new ships, their trade declined steadily from about 1877. By 1885 the position of the older dock systems and the laborers dependent on them had become desperate.

All of London suffered a continuous economic deterioration from 1870 to 1914. With the collapse of its three major industries, this decline in East London began earlier and was more severe than in the rest of the metropolitan area. The recurring depressions (1866-67, 1879, and 1884-87) only added to the personal suffering. From the mid-eighteen-fifties until the First World War, East London's economic base was declining while at the same time it was experiencing a rapid increase of population. Those factors, together with the shrinking availability of housing and rising rents, combined to produce the slums of East London in the Victorian era.

Reactions to the Slum

There was no other large slum area of the nineteenth or any earlier century that attracted as much public notice as East London. Literally hundreds of contemporary accounts have survived. not counting the multitude of parliamentary investigations, Sanitary Inspectors' reports, and poor Law Commission inquiries. What distinguishes these accounts is that they were all composed by people who were, more or less, outsiders. Dyos has noted that the modern researcher misses any mention of the "bodily sensations" or the emotional reactions engendered by slum life. "The fact is," he writes, "that the annals of the urban poor are buried deeper than those of the rural poor and the London poor perhaps deepest of all." [16] Fortunately Mayhew collected his classic accounts of the London poor a generation before "scientific" investigation and the amassing of statistics came into vogue. There were others. Writing in the same year as Mayhew, John Hollingshead described a house, neither better nor worse than its neighbors, in St. George's-in-the-East:

> The ground floor . . . is occupied by a sweep. A short
> broom sticks out over the door. The front parlour con-
> tains two women, half covered with soot. A bed, as
> black as the women, stands in the corner, in which an in-

> fant is sleeping, with its little face looking pale even un-
> der the dirt, and its head lying lower than its legs. Six
> other children, belonging to the same parents, are playing
> somewhere about in the inky puddles [outdoors] . . . .
> Upstairs, in one room, is a street hawker, with a wife and
> five children, and in another room is a carpenter, also
> with a wife and five children. . . . When they are gathered
> together at night--if they are ever so gathered--the roof of
> this stunted dwelling will cover twenty-five inmates. [17]

It is a depressing but not an atypical picture. Most houses in East London were very much like this one, with "two rooms up and two rooms
down." Few families, with the exception of tradesmen who kept a store
downstairs, had a whole building to themselves. Normally, such a house
was occupied by two families. But in the poorest districts, six different
familes, including as many as fifty individuals, squeezed into the same
small space.

The grimness of such a view can be overstressed, however.
There were as least pockets of a residual middle class sprinkled throughout East London, even at the end of the nineteenth century. Certain
tradesmen, especially publicans, were prosperous. And some contemporary observers, such as Harry Jones, the Rector of St. George's-in-the-
East, argued that East London was not nearly as appalling as was often
claimed. Having recently come from a wealthy parish in Westminster,
he wrote that one of his first impressions was ". . . of the nearness of the
East of London to the West. The East is, to many who dwell in the
West, an unknown distant land." He noted the "spaciousness" of East
London, couplimented its "cosmopolitan" tenor, and argued that much
worse slums were to be found in the West. Even allowing for a natural
defensiveness about his parish's reputation, Jones saw curiously little
poverty around him. The furthest he would go was to admit, "The East
of London is conspicuous for its preponderance of poor or working people." [18] In one sense Jones was certainly right. A few years later his
friend Samuel Barnett would complain that West End visitors to Whitechapel frequently expressed disappointment at not seeing greater poverty.

But on the whole, Jones' vision was clouded by his laudable desire to defend his parishioners against widespread disbelief in their humanity.

Jones had much to contend against. Thomas Huxley, not an
inconsiderable figure, believed East London a suitable area for anthropo-
logical investigation: "I have seen the Polynesian savage, in his primi-
tive condition, before the missionary or the blackbirder [slavetrader] or
the beach-comber got at him. With all his savagery, he was not half so
savage, so unclean, so irreclaimable, as the tenant of a tenement in an
East London slum." [19] Walter Besant, the well-known novelist, was
closely involved with East London for twenty-five years before his death
in 1901. His own view was somewhere between those of Jones and
Huxley, but it could not be called chauvinistic. He spoke of East London as "the Unlovely City", "the City of Dreadful Monotony", and a city
with "no history." East London, Besant wrote, lacked all the characteris-
tics usually associated with city life. It had no center, no fashionable
quarter, no representative body, no mayor, no public or high schools, no
bookshops or periodicals. "People, shops, houses, conveyances--all together are stamped with the unmistakable seal of the working class . . .
perhaps the strangest thing of all is this: in a city of two million people
there are no hotels! That means, of course, that there are no visitors."
But even if he found the amenities of urban life missing, Besant was
quick to defend East London against charges of being one unrelieved
slum: ". . . it is not a city of slums, but of respectability." [20] There
were slums, he admitted, but they did not define the character of the
place.

The "respectability" of East London is the one quality most
often forgotten in both contemporary and later discussions of the area.
The residents were not unsocialized barbarians, notwithstanding Huxley.
For the most part they were natives of the region, participants in a genuine Cockney subculture. They shared traditions, rituals, and to some extent a dialect that was foreign to their fellow-countrymen. Mayhew has
outlined this subculture accurately: its elaborate systems of credit, its in-
tense loyalties, its "slang language", its public houses. There was a respectability that went with being a Cockney, even a poor Cockney. The
common English failure to admit the validity of this subculture has resulted, during both Victorian and later times, in too easy a dismissal of

East London as a hopeless parasite on the rest of the city.

After 1860, however, Huxley's view was in the ascent. As middle-class Englishmen discovered the new phenomenon of the urban slum, their primary reaction was one of fear. The values of their nation had always been rooted in the village, not the city. The paternalistic tie between squire and laborer, the moral influence of the church, a politics based on face-to-face relationships. all these seemed threatened by the new industrial order. and most of all by the industrial slum. The Chartist uprisings of the thirties and forties had been the signal that something was dangerously wrong in English society. Disraeli speculated about the "two nations" that existed side-by-side on one small island. Throughout the Victorian period, the middle-class nation feared, and had reason to fear, that it might eventually be overwhelmed by the new nation growing up alongside it.

As the century progressed, these middle-class fears came increasingly to focus on East London. In part, this was a natural development, for London was the metropolis, by far the largest city in the world, and East London claimed the greatest expanse of slum dwellings on the European continent. But in part this focusing was due also to a decline of working-class agitation in the northern cities after the waning of Chartism. Particularly in Manchester there developed institutions among the largely dissenting laborers that stressed sobriety, self-help, and discipline. [21]   But no parallel institutions evolved in London until the end of the century. From about 1850 until the end of Victoria's reign, therefore, East London served as the *locus classicus* of the urban slum, a feared, repellent, but nonetheless fascinating, land.

G. S. Jones has written of this fascination for the slum:

> The poor districts became an immense *terra incognita*
> periodically mapped out by intrepid missionaries and ex-
> plorers who catered to an insatiable middle-class demand
> for travellers' tales. These writers sometimes expressed
> apprehension about the large and anonymous proletarian
> areas of South London, but the most extensive and the
> most feared area was the East End, a huge city itself in all
> but name. [22]

Beginning about 1880, the term "East End" came into general use, a dramatic way of symbolizing one of Disraeli's "two nations." The term was pejorative, indicating "a different world, an unknown world, within the same city." But at least it suggested that the East and West Ends were parts of a single whole, dependent on one another and jointly responsible for the welfare of the metropolis. With all the discussions of the "social problem", that underlying unity had been nearly forgotten. Asa Briggs speaks of the distinction between the two regions as "the great contrast of the 1880s and 1890s." [23] This was particularly true during the 1884-87 depression, when the desperate plight of many East Enders was widely publicized by the press. An epidemic of "slumming" followed. Partly from a real desire to help, partly to satisfy their own voyeuristic curiosity, fashionable West Enders descended on the East. Sinclair writes: "Slumming became part of the education, and sometimes even the sport, of well-to-do men and women. Groups of young women accompanied by their maids would visit East London and try to bridge the yawning gap between the two worlds" [24] It was rarely a successful attempt, but it did have some good effects. It increased national attention on the slums, resulting in more money and personnel being directed to social work in the area. Indeed, the prominence of the East end engendered some resentment in London's other slum areas. Charles Booth noted at the turn of the century:

> The last twenty-five or thirty years have seen the rise of a
> number of great organisations aimed at the amelioration
> of the conditions of life in East London, and the moral
> and spiritual advancement of its people. So largely have
> these efforts been concentrated upon this particular district
> of London, that elsewhere it is often regarded as receiving
> more than its share. "We are just as poor" (we hear it said
> rather bitterly), "but our poverty excites no such interest.
> We are not the 'East End'." [25]

By the 1900s the East End had become not only England's best-known slum area, but also the source of models for understanding urban poverty and a laboratory for social experiments. It was from the East End that C.

G. Masterman derived his famous image of the "nether world" over which
the middle classes travelled on their elevated railways between their suburban homes and their posts in the City. [26]

Charles Booth and the East End

It was inevitable, given the scientific spirit of the late Victorian age, that someone should press beyond metaphors, beyond slumming,
beyond partial or impressionistic accounts, to attempt a systematic survey of East End poverty. That man was Charles Booth. Born in 1840 to
a successful Unitarian family, he had made a fortune in shipping by the
time he moved to London in the early eighteen-eighties. Once in the metropolis he felt a romantic pull to the East End, often roaming its streets,
occasionally renting a room for himself in one of the shabbier neighborhoods. He came to admire the poor for what he saw as their strength.
their spontaneity, and their almost Darwinian struggle against great odds.
Then, in 1885, the **Pall Mall Gazette** published the results of a limited survey of London poverty attempted by the marxist Social Democratic
Federation. It was a natural cause for the **Gazette**, a muck-raking newspaper under the editorship of the socially reformist W. T. Stead. Booth,
with his admiration for East Enders, doubted the survey's results, which
indicated that one Londoner out of every four lived in abject destitution.
He determined to undertake a study of his own. His original intentions
were modest, but his project was not. It would take seventeen years and
result in the seventeen volumes of **Life and Labour of the People
in London**, still the classic survey of urban Poverty.

Booth recruited a number of volunteers, most notably the
young Beatrice Potter, his cousin by marriage and later the wife of Sidney Webb. Together they determined that, at least initially, they would
not carry out any independent investigations, but would rely on statistics
already gathered by others, particularly the house-to-house visitation reports of the various London School Boards. Using these reports, Booth
first analyzed the "inner circle" of the East End, where the bulk of East
London's poverty was to be found. Beyond this quadrant, further to the

north and east, lay the developing middle-class "suburbs" of the nineteenth century. When his correlations were completed, Booth professed himself appalled by what he had shown: more than one-third of the nearly one million East Londoners were "poor", a proportion that rose to nearly one-half in the worst districts. Booth's figures very nearly caused a sensation.

Life and Labour became a cause for Booth and his investigators. As they continued their survey to include all of London, they discovered that just over thirty percent of the city's residents fell at or below the poverty level. The result amazed Booth and most contemporary observers. Poverty was not, as had been thought, confined to the east and the south, for some of London's worst privation was to be found in small pockets scattered throughout the West End. The East End, however, did retain its primacy as the one region of the metropolitan area where poverty was the dominant mode of life. Booth wrote, "On the whole it will be seen that St. George's-in-the-East is the poorest district , though run very hard by Bethnal Green in this unenviable race." [27]

Despite his inherited bias against the Church of England, Booth hoped that the Established Church might somehow reverse the decline. The third series of his study focused on "religious influences". It constituted very nearly a parish-by-parish survey of the churchesand chapelsin London, few receiving more than two or three paragraphs apiece- In Iarge measure, these seven additional volumes added very little, They were too quickly researched and too impressionistic to be of much value. But they did point up one fact: the Anglican Church was thriving in middle-class neighborhoods, while its influence. with very few exceptions, was either nonexistent or even negative in the poorer districts. Booth came away from his study in 1903 depressed about both the future of London's slums and the improving power of religion. But that was at the end of the Victorian era. At the beginning of the reign it was not at all clear what the church could do in the slums, for until then it had hardly tried. The urban slum was to be one of the great challenges faced bY the Victorian church.

The Church in the East End

The Church of England was not in a healthy condition when Victoria came to the throne. The lassitude of the early nineteenth century clergy and the corresponding prevalence of fox-hunting parsons has probably been exaggerated, but the caricature points to an underlying truth. Robert Gregory, an outstanding slum clergyman in Lambeth and later Dean of St. Paul's, has recorded a typical story from the period:

> ... the present Archbishop of Canterbury, Dr. [Frederick] Temple, told me that when he was a young man [ca. 1840] he attended St. Paul's one Sunday morning, intending to remain for Holy Communion. When the earlier part of the service was over, a virger [sic] came to him and said, 'I hope, sir, you are not intending to remain for the sacrament, as that will give the Minor Canon the trouble of celebrating, which otherwise he will not do. [28]

In the East End, the situation was even worse. Few of the incumbents were resident in their parishes, some only coming from their West End homes to take Sunday services, the more energetic employing young curates to do the pastoral work. Pluralism was often the rule. As late as the eighteen-fifties, the Rector of St. Matthew's, Bethnal Green, lived at his other parish in Cheshire, while the Rector of St. Dunstan's was rarely seen in his medieval church. [29] Most of the resident clergy were either lazy or incompetent or both. Bryan King, who began his East End ministry in 1837, often told the story of a neighboring incumbent who was remonstrated by the bishop for reportedly keeping a cask of beer on tap in his study. "A cask of **beer**, my lord!", he replied, "I should like to know the author of this monstrous scandal. I venture to say that it is a cask of as good **ale** as was ever brewed." [30]

There were some good reasons for this paucity of active clergy in the East End. All parsons, but particularly those of the Established Church, were subject to harassment in the streets. Even if a clergyman were willing to tolerate popular opposition, it was often not safe for his wife and children to live in the area. But there were bad reasons, as well.

Until the middle of the century, most churchmen assumed that the poor were divinely ordered to their estate. Even John Keble, one of the great Victorian pastors, argued that, "God has divided the world into rich and poor, that there might be more exercise of charity and patience." [31] It was not a vision that tended to inspire young clergymen with thoughts of what they might accomplish in slum parishes, As long as charity was considered the only response to a static social order, the East End churches would not attract the active and reformist clergy that might turn them into missionary outposts.

But the generation after Victoria's accession witnessed the beginning of two great changes in the Church of England. The first was a revival of idealism in the parochial ministry. It was almost universally recognized by at least 1860: "Mid-Victorian churchmen, high, low and broad, looked back to the eighteenth century and to the early years of their own century as a time when the parishes were manned by lax and indifferent clergy .... All felt that they lived in an era of clerical renaissance, when the profession of which they were members had been given a new life." [32]   Most observers correctly trace this rebirth to both the evangelical and anglo-catholic movements- As the two religious revivals increasingly swept up both low and high churchmen, the universities began to turn out young men fired with a clerical idealism that had not been typical in the Church of England for a century and a half. In many ways, it was the age of great parish clergymen, and it had its effect upon the East End. Walter Besant, no enthusiast for the Establishment, noted: "There is at the present moment [1901] no more active clergy in the world than our own; there is no organization more complete than that of a well worked London parish. The young men who now take Holy Orders know, at the outset, that they must lead lives of perpetual activity." [33] Chadwick believes that by the middle of the century, the "devotional appeal" of slum parishes was universally recognized. [34] Perhaps he has anticipated slightly, for it was not until the mid-eighteen-sixties that the shortage of faithful clergy in the East End finally eased. Nevertheless, his point is correct: during the later years of the Victorian era the East End was no longer marked by clerical indolence, for it had begun to attract some of the church's ablest young clergy.

The other change is harder to specify: it is the gradual permea-
tion of the whole Church of England by F. D. Maurice's social idealism.
Much of Maurice's thought was centered on the poor and on how the
church might minister to them. In 1851 he wrote: "There are not at
present many [clergymen] (I have no doubt there will be soon a great
number) who feel as strongly as I do, that, unless we on our side strive
heart and soul to show the working classes that the Church is their best
friend, and is ready to make every sacrifice for their sake, we shall not
only lose all hold over them, but over the upper classes to which we
have sacrificed them." [35] Maurice proved, as he so often did, a good
prophet. By the end of the century prominent churchmen of every party
shared, if not Maurice's theology, at least his concern for the poor. Keble's belief that charity was the only Christian answer to social inequality
was swept aside in the generation after his death. Historians have largely
focused on the confluence of Maurician theology and anglo-catholicism
by the century's end. But this debate has obscured the much broader influence Maurice exerted throughout and even beyond the church. By the
eighteen-eighties Maurice's thought had become part of the heritage of
the English church, a heritage with which any candidate in theology at
Oxford or Cambridge would have had to be familiar. By 1902 Bishop W.
E. Collins could say of Maurice: "many elements in his teaching have
been so generally assimilated among us that this very fact stands in the
way of our realizing our debt to him; we neither know whence we derived
them nor who it was who brought them forth, but assume that our fa-
thers were as familiar with them as we are." [36]

This new idealism about parish ministry in general and about
the ministry to the working classes in particular was shaken, as the
whole nation was shaken, by the Religious Census of 1851. The government of Lord John Russell determined to collect statistics of church attendance in conjunction with the normal census scheduled for that year.
An agent, Horace Mann, was employed to manage the project. He attempted to amass attendance figures for every church and chapel in England and Wales on a single Sunday, 30 March 1851. It was not an entirely accurate survey, first because the date of the enumeration was known
several weeks in advance, second because some attendants were counted at
both morning and evening services, third because not every minister

agreed to co-operate, and fourth because Mann had no way to check the accuracy of the voluntarily returned forms. But it was the first religious census of its kind, and even though its results were widely attacked, it caused something of a sensation. [37]

Mann's principal conclusion, and the one that attracted most attention, was that the majority of a population numbering nearly eighteen million did not attend religious worship of any kind on the chosen Sunday. Even allowing for those who had to work on Sundays, for the sick and infirm and for those who had to care for them, Mann estimated that more than five million able-bodied people chose not to attend church. In 1851 this was regarded as a momentous discovery, challenging the Victorian conviction that Britain was a Christian nation. But even more threatening was the social distribution of church attendance. What had earlier been only dimly perceived was now clearly demonstrated: the Church of England was the church of the middle and upper classes. The urban laborers, by and large, were estranged from every religious body. This was true in all the "chief manufacturing districts", but it was particularly noticeable in London. The percentage of metropolitan residents attending church was lower than that in any other city. Among London's eight parliamentary districts it was lowest of all in the Borough of Tower Hamlets. Just under thirty percent of East End residents attended worship, and a bare majority of those went to dissenting churches. The Religious Census of 1851 became a watershed, demonstrating for the first time the Church of England's near-total failure among the urban working-class. Mann's dry statistics constituted a call for the idealistic young clergy to go into the slums. The Establishment, no less than the vision of a Christian nation, was at stake.

The Religious Census proved that parts of England were no less a missionary field than the colonies. After 1853 calls to the "home mission" became more frequent, diverting an ever-larger number of young clergy who might earlier have been drawn into the foreign missions. This was particularly true among Anglicans, for Mann's figures showed, to nearly everyone's astonishment, that only a bare majority of worshippers attended their local parishes. Nearly half of England's church-going Christians were Roman Catholics, Presbyterians, Methodists, Congregationalists, or Baptists. The old assumptions that underlay the Establishment were in danger. This was not surprising in East London, for that area had been a fertile ground for dissenters since at least the mid-seventeenth century. Stepney had by then acquired a Puritan reputation that was only enhanced by the immigration of the Huguenots. But the Census showed that in many northern cities, an even smaller proportion of the worshipping laborers attended Anglican services. The obvious conclusion was that the Church of England was imperiled. A mission to the slum was essential not just to save the poor from the fate of the unchurched; it was essential, as well, to save the Establishment.

One of Mann's principal areas of investigation has received scant attention in the later literature. That concerned the number of parochial "sittings" available to serve the rapidly expanding industrial areas of the nation. The Church of England had pointed with pride to its construction of more than two thousand churches in the twenty years between 1831 and 1851. Mann, however, concluded that the great majority of these edifices had been built in the new, middle-class suburban areas. "It is to satisfy the wants of these two [middle and upper] classes that the number of religious structures has of late years been so increased." What was needed, he argued, were at least two thousand more church structures concentrated "in the **large town districts** of the country,--more especially in London." [38] If only the Church of England could provide a sufficient number of parishes and free (i.e., unrented) pews in the slums, Mann believed, the trend of the urban working class away from the Established Church might be reversed.

The Bishop of London had anticipated Mann's faith in church building. When Charles James Blomfield came to the diocese in 1828, there were only nine parishes to serve all of East London. Two were medieval foundations: St. Dunstan's, Stepney, and St. Mary Matfelon, Whitechapel. Two more had been built in the seventeenth century along the increasingly populous riverside: St. John's, Wapping, and St. Paul's, Shadwell. Finally, five more had been added in the eighteenth century, all under the aegis of the "Fifty Churches Act" of 1711: St. Mary's, Bow; Christ Church, Spitalfields; St. George's-in-the-East; St. Anne's Limehouse; and St. Matthew's, Bethnal Green. [39] These nine parishes had to minister to a population of more than a quarter million. While the riverfront was relatively well served, the interior of the East End had only five parishes, each covering a vast area: one in Whitechapel, one in Spitalfields, one in Bethnal Green, one in Stepney, and one outside East London's inner circle in Bow. Blomfield, the outstanding episcopal administrator of the nineteenth century, saw his work in the East End as hopeless unless he could build at least a dozen more churches in the area. He was to fulfill his goal.

Blomfield placed his inital hopes in the Church Building Commissioners, established by the 1818 "Act for Building and Promoting the Building of Additional Churches in Populous parishes." The Commissioners were well-intentioned, setting careful guidelines to ensure that a substantial portion of each new church's seats would be free for poorer worshippers, but they quickly exhausted their Parliamentary grants of 1818 and 1824, building only one new church in the East End, Christ Church, Watney Street, consecrated in 1841. Blomfield, however, was only momentarily deterred.

Because he could not get more money from parliament, and because he was prevented from redistributing the scandalous emoluments of St. Paul's and the City's wealthiest benefices, Blomfield went directly to the public. In 1836 he established the Metropolis Churches' Fund, issued an appeal for donations, and formed a committee under the King's patronage to administer the contributions. The response was immediate, more than a hundred thousand pounds coming in the first year alone. The committee took its work seriously, investigating the adequacy of each existing parish, deciding on a standard of one church for every three thousand people, and setting an inital goal of fifty new parishes, most to be built in the poorer districts of the diocese. Two of the first churches it supported were in the East End: St. James, Ratcliff, and St. Peter's, Cephas Street, both consecrated in 1838. In 1854 the M.C.F. was reconstituted as the Bishop of London's Fund, and as such it continued its work of building almost unabated until 1880. There was never really any hope that the Fund could meet its standard of one church for every three thousand people. That would have meant almost three hundred new parishes at the time the Fund was established, and the population of London would more than double by the end of the century. Nonetheless, the effect on the East End was dramatic. Between 1836 and 1900, forty new parishes were built in the area, bringing the total from nine to forty-nine in little more than two generations. Most of these new churches were at least aided by the Fund. The old parish of Bethnal Green was subdivided into fourteen parochial districts, Whitechapel into nine, and St. George's-in-the-East into six. [40] It seemed that Bishop Blomfield's and Horace Mann's hopes for new churches in the poorer areas were being at least approached, if not fulfilled, in the East End.

But church-building alone was not to prove a sufficient answer to the Church of England's failure in the slums. At the time of the 1851 Religious Census, and presumably earlier as well, most of the urban poor never ventured into the churches. To be effective, the clergy of the new parishes would have to assume a missionary stance, challenging much of the Established Church's inherited thinking, developing new styles of ministry. Whether they could succeed or not was very much an open question at the beginning of Victoria's reign.

II

THE ANGLO-CATHOLICS

Edward B. Pusey, the leader of the Tractarians after Newman's defection, wrote in an 1855 letter, "If I had no duties here, and had fluency, I would long ago have asked leave to preach in the alleys of London, where the Gospel is as unknown as in Tibet." [1] Pusey did go to the East End, but only for an occasional preaching mission; it was his younger followers who went and stayed there. Owen Chadwick speaks of seven as outstanding: "Mackonochie, Lowder, Dolling, Stanton, Suckling, Russell, Wainright, came through to the imagination of the poor." [2] But Chadwick is unusually comprehensive. Only the first four names are invoked by most historians; they are the undisputed heroes of the movement. Two things are notable about this list: first, with the exception of Dolling, all these men were associated with just two parishes, St. Alban's Holborn, and St. Peter's, London Docks; and second, the former of these is not even located in the East End. Yet the power of historical myth-making being what it is, St. Alban's is often assimilated to East London, and these two parishes have been generalized into a movement. In his recent book A. Tindal Hart is being more faithful to mythology than to history when he writes; "The Anglo-Catholics in particular were the champions of the workers; and slum curates in the East End of London and elsewhere were conspicuous for getting the poor to attend their churches by the combination of a colourful ritualism with a fiery socialism." [3]

This is not to say that the anglo-catholics were absent from the slums. Taking the use of eucharistic vestments as a standard of catholic practice, slightly more than one-third of the East End parishes were anglo-catholic by the turn of the century, compared with slightly less than one-quarter of the parishes in England as a whole. [4] But of all the anglo-catholic parishes in the East End, only St. Peter's, London Docks, had the character of a mission. The others had small staffs, usually just one or two priests, and were largely undistinguished in either influence or attendance from their neighboring parishes. In fact, of all the anglo-catholic parishes in the East End, only St. Peter's, London Docks, had an attendance in 1902 and 1903 that far outstripped the mean for its borough. The **Daily News** survey conducted during those years concluded that the anglo-catholic parishes in the poorer sections of the city were not nearly as strong as had been expected:

> The High Church--or at least the Ritualist section of the
> High Church--does not seem to have made the progress
> that everybody anticipated. Here and there an able, devot-
> ed man has built up a strong and flourishing church, but
> there are many instances of ineffectiveness and incapacity.
> [5]

The anglo-catholics established a proud record of service in the East End. But they were not so uniformly distinguished as a party, nor were they so uniquely successful in attracting the poor, as many historians of the Church of England have maintained.

By far the best known and the most influential East End anglo- catholic was Charles Fuge Lowder, founder of St. George's mission and later Vicar of St. Peter's, London Docks. In his own day he was an enormously popular figure. His biography, first published a year after his death, ran to fourteen editions. But despite the constant reference to him as the pre-eminent East End ritualist, despite the considerable volume of records he left behind, despite the parish's efforts to keep his memory alive (St. Peter's still observes the day of his death, September 9th, as a feast day), he has remained until now very much an unstudied figure. In part this is due to the comprehensiveness of that early biography. But in part the neglect is probably due also to Lowder's somewhat forbidding character. He was reserved, moralistic, selfless in his service, and profoundly clerical. Yet the passage of nearly one hundred years is perhaps beginning to moderate that aloofness. Lowder is the subject of a recent book, and his life was made the special essay topic for students doing the 1976 A-level examinations in religion at the Wolverhampton comprehensive schools. [6]

In many ways, Lowder's background was typical for an anglo-catholic of his generation. Born at Bath in 1820 to successful, even wealthy parents, he had been raised with old-fashioned high-church principles. In 1840 he entered Exeter College, Oxford, just at the height of tensions aroused by the Oxford Movement. Here he witnessed the storm that followed the publication of **Tract 90,** Isaac Williams' failure to obtain the Professorship of Poetry, and Pusey's suspension for his sermon on the eucharist. He became a partisan of Newman, attending all his sermons, and visiting the great man after his retirement to Littlemore. There seems never to have been any doubt that he would take orders. Immediately after receiving his degree, with second class honors in classics, he was ordained to a rural parish near Glastonbury, in his home diocese of Bath and Wells. Soon, however, his responsibilities increased when his father's bank failed and his parents became nearly impoverished. Lowder moved to a second curacy at Tetbury, in the diocese of Gloucester, which provided a house large enough for him to accommodate his family. A distinct anglo-catholic, he did as much as a curate could to advance the ritual of the two parishes. Briefly he flirted with going into the foreign mission field, either in New Zealand or in South Africa, but on each occasion he was blocked by concern for his family. It seemed inevitable that Lowder would advance to a quiet rural incumbency.

But he was frustrated by the liturgical conservatism of his parish. Later he was to write of himself in the third person; "He felt that in his own parish he had reached the end of his tether: after nearly six years of parochial labour he could not induce his vicar to move further in advance, and St. Barnabas offered a most inviting field for more congenial work." [7] St. Barnabas, in the London district of Pimlico, had been built in 1850 by W. J. E. Bennett to serve the poorest area in the parish of St. Paul's , Knightsbridge. From the first it had been a Tractarian establishment. Its ritual was in advance of any other London church of the time, it was the first church in London whose pews were entirely free, and it was the only such church to separate men from women in the congregation. It was natural that Lowder and St. Barnabas should come together. Making other arrangements for his family, the Tetbury curate wrote the new vicar in Pimlico: "My opinions are perhaps best expressed, as we must use terms of distinction in these days, by the name of Anglo-Catholic, being decidedly those of firm attachment to the Church of England, with the earnest hope of being an humble instrument in bringing her Catholic character more closely home to the heart of her members." [8]

Lowder at St. Barnabas

Lowder served at St. Barnabas for five, litigious years during which controversy with Bishop Blomfield was continual. One Parishioner, Charles Westerton, supported almost constant legal action against the church's ritual. The use of a stone altar, colored altar cloths, crosses, lighted candles, the eastward position, and stoles seemed radical at the time. One of Westerton's complaints alleged the lack of tablets bearing the Ten Commandments to be a serious fault. These legal maneuvers were eventually to result in the first great court victory for the anglo-catholics: the 1857 "Knightsbridge Judgement" of the privy Council's Judicial Committee, affirming that liturgical ornaments used at the time of the first Book of Common prayer (1549) were still legal in the Church of England. Two events that helped shape Lowder's future occurred during the years at St. Barnabas. The first began with a trivial incident that did him little credit. In 1854 Westerton, who was then running for the post of churchwarden, hired a placard-bearer to carry his campaign sign about the parish. Lowder's eleven-year-old cousin, together with some of the parish choir boys, came to him with plans for a counter-attack. Foolishly, Lowder provided them with money to purchase rotten eggs, missiles that were subsequently put to good use. Lowder was arrested but immediately released upon admission of guilt. The Bishop, who seemed amused by the incident, felt that stronger action was called for. He suspended Lowder for six weeks. Westerton, perhaps unwittingly aided by Lowder, won the election.

Mortified, Lowder resolved to go abroad, probably to escape from his embarrassing situation, but probably also to see at first hand the workings of the Roman Catholic Church. While in England, an Anglican priest was cut off from even casual contacts with Roman Catholics. But on the Continent, far away from the Church of England, there was no such restraint. It is probable that Lowder had been planning such a trip for some time; his suspension merely gave him the opportunity. [9] Lowder's contemporary John Mason Neale, the anglo-catholic hymn translator, had planned to accompany him, but begged off because of duties at East Grinstead. Thus Lowder travelled alone to Le Havre and from there--largely on foot--to Rouen and finally to Yvetot, where he stayed at the Petit Séminaire, a Roman Catholic school for boys. There he developed a friendship with the priest-superior, F. L. Labbé, who gave him a copy of Louis Abelly's **Vie de Saint Vincent de Paul**. The book, so Lowder later recalled, was to change his life: "No one can read this interesting Biography without the deepest interest, and the heart must be dull indeed which is not stirred with emotion at the self-denial and energy with which the Saint gave himself to the work to which he was called." [10] To Lowder it seemed that the Victorian Church of England faced many of the same problems Vincent de Paul had encountered: Widespread poverty, indifference to religion, unspiritual clergy. The answer, he thought, might be a group of priests working along the lines of the Vincentian order, devoted to the principles outlined in Abelly's book: 1) that each priest should work for his own perfection, 2) that they should preach the gospel to the poor, and 3) that they should help train ordinands in the knowledge and the virtues required by the priesthood. [11] Upon returning to England Lowder wrote Labbé, asking for a copy of the constitution of the Vincentians, but the French priest replied, with regret, that he had never owned a copy. Apparently Lowder never did see the constitution, but he determined that something like Vincentian service to the poor was his own vocation.

The second important event during his St. Barnabas years was the founding of the Society of the Holy Cross in early 1855. The Society (always referred to as the S.S.C. after its Latin title, Societas Sanctae Crucis) seems to have been a direct outgrowth of Lowder's encounter with Abelly's biography. Certainly Lowder was its chief instigator, the S.S.C. was founded shortly after his return from France, and the Society's historian affirmed the connection. From its beginning the Society focused on clerical devotion and behavior, attempting to provide a Continental form of "priestly formation" absent in the Church of England.

These were not its only concerns, however. In 1856 it held the first retreat in the Church of England. By 1858 the retreats had taken an Ignatian form and had become a regular part of the Society's life. Shortly thereafter the S.S.C. began to experiment with parochial missions, one and two week pastoral efforts that concentrated on preaching, confession, and rededication. Both of these--the retreats and the parish missions--were eventually adopted by evangelicals, as well. Most importantly, the S.S.C., in its earliest years, supported the foundation of the St. George's Mission.

One of the Society's first goals had been "establishing home missions amongst the masses of our working population." [12] In January 1856 the members began approaching anglo-catholic vicars of large slum parishes in London, asking whether they would welcome such a

mission within their districts. Bryan King, overwhelmed by his responsibility for 30,000 poor parishioners, offered his parish, St. George's-in-
the-East. Beginning on Ash Wednesday 1856, therefore, the S.S.C. began a mission in the East End. Three evenings a week, first in the parish
schoolrooms and then in a rented room in Wapping, the Society's priests
held short missionary services consisting of hymns, a sermon, and
prayers. The inadequacy of such an effort was quickly apparent. King
wanted Lowder to undertake a permanent mission under his direction but
Lowder insisted, as a precondition, that the proposed mission be independent of the Rector's authority. The dispute was submitted to Pusey for
mediation, but the question of jurisdiction was never entirely solved. Despite this unresolved issue, the S.S.C. decided in June to make the Mission a permanent foundation, with Lowder as its first head.

What is remarkable is the speed with which the Mission took
shape. Money was raised, a house was purchased in the center of Wapping, a chapel of prefabricated iron was constructed in its garden, and
Lowder, together with another S.S.C. priest, took up residence, all by
the end of 1856. The "Iron Chapel" was dedicated in November as the
Chapel of the Good Shepherd. Early the next year another sphere of activity was added. A disused Danish Lutheran Church in Wellclose Square,
just one quarter mile west of St. George's-in-the-East, was rented, refurbished, and dedicated as St. Saviour's. Two clergy, together with several
lay assistants, moved into the new district. Meanwhile, Lowder invited
Elizabeth Neale, sister of John Mason Neale, to found a sisterhood in
conjunction with the Mission. Within a few months two women had
joined her and the Community of the Holy Cross was begun. By the end
of 1857, therefore, just a year and a half after its inauguration, the Mission had very nearly assumed its final character. Though Lowder's biog-
raphers praise him principally for his indefatigable labors and for his personal holiness, he must have been a remarkable administrator, as well.

The Mission Staff

From the beginning, the Mission's worship was more ritualistic than that of any contemporary London church. The eucharist was celebrated daily with vestments and lighted candles. Soon incense was added
on Sundays and other festivals. Confession was taught and practiced.
Lowder and the other clergy wanted to be called "Father," and within ten

years the address had become common parlance within the district. The Mission was extreme in its Roman tendences, and the 1859 to 1861 "no-popery" riots at St. George's only increased Lowder's resolve. That he was not made the object of ritual persecutions, by either protestant mobs or legal action, must have been partly due to the obscurity of both Wapping and Wellclose Square. But it was also a testament to Lowder's uncombative resolve. Firm, even rigid, in his ritualistic convictions, he was nonetheless capable of winning the respect of his opponents, even that of the bishop. The word for Lowder is "solid." No one doubted his loyalty to the Church of England or his commitment to parochial work. Lowder entirely lacked that mark of romantic instability so obvious in many of his anglo-catholic colleagues. His former superior at St. Barnabas wrote of him after his death: "No man had less of mere aesthetic sentiment about his religion. He was weak, rather than otherwise, in imaginative power; but he had considerable intellectual, specially logical, force, and a strong will, combined with indomitable courage." [13] Neither a visionary nor a romantic, Lowder's notes were labor and self-discipline. Apparently he never even considered becoming a Roman Catholic. A derivative rather than a creative thinker, his theology came from Pusey, just as his ritual came from what he conceived to be the standard of the western church, the Roman rite. In the Mission's early years, he rarely left the East End except for S.S.C. meetings. Even in the years before his death, when he was forced by declining health to spend months at a time recuperating in the country, he rarely preached outside his own parish. Though he died at a comparatively young age in 1880, he was among that small group of intensely committed anglo-catholic clergy who, by their almost total dedication to parochial service, helped redeem their whole movement from charges of instability and disloyalty.

Initially, Lowder had hoped that the Mission clergy would evolve into a religious order somewhat like the Vincentians. He alluded to this hope frequently, as when he wrote, "The idea of the Priests of the Mission living together in community was the very essence of the Mission." [14] But only once, in his "Annual Report for 1862", did he make that expectation explicit: "At the very commencement of the Mission it was hoped that a body of clergy and laymen living together in a religious house might form the nucleus of a monastic order in the Church of England." [15] Had Lowder succeeded, it would have been the first Anglican religious community of men. He tried strenuously; the regimen in the clergy house was strictly monastic. But Lowder's failure must certainly have been due to the rapid turn-over in curates. It would be fifteen years before Lowder could achieve anything resembling a stable college connected with the Mission. For the first ten years he rarely had more than two ordained assistants, and frequently he was reduced to only one. The annual reports for that period are filled with appeals for clerical help; that for 1863 is typical: "Two Priests and a Deacon are now endeavouring to fulfil the duties which require, at least, two more Clergy." [16] In part the problem was probably financial. Even twenty years later, when the Mission was well established and comparatively well financed, the curates received only fifty pounds a year. The austerity of Mission life may well have been another factor. But perhaps the principal difficulty was that service in the Mission might well torpedo a young clergyman's future career. Until almost 1870 it was not at all certain that the Mission would succeed. Clerical unemployment was no more inviting a prospect one hundred years ago than it is today.

The lack of clergy would not have been such a serious problem had not several seceded to Roman Catholicism. St. George's Mission faced the same crisis that undermined almost every other anglo-catholic experiment. The first secessions came in 1857. The Mission had seemed in good health by the middle of that year. Lowder had four assistants: three priests, one of them temporary, and a layman. At the end of the year, however, the two permanent priests and the layman resigned to join the Roman Church. William W. Champneys, the evangelical Vicar of St. Mary Matfelon, Whitechapel, wrote Bishop Tait to request that Lowder's license be withdrawn, at least for work in the Wellclose Square district. Somehow Tait's hand was stayed, but the continuance of the Mission seemed momentarily in doubt.

Lowder, whose own health was near the breaking point, wrote bravely: "Under such circumstances it cannot be supposed, that the Mission work could be maintained with the same vigour as when there were four clergy devoting themselves to the care of souls and visiting in the District." [17] But the Mission's survival was assured a year later when Alexander Mackonochie left Wantage and came to work alongside Lowder. The two men proved an ideal pair. Only five years the vicar's junior, an active member of the S.S.C. sharing his view of the church, the new curate brought about ". . . what might be called a revival." [18] Mackonochie took total charge of the Wellclose Square district, leaving Lowder free to concentrate his whole attention upon Wapping. Despite the St. George's riots, despite their having to staff two chapels with little assistance, the Mission prospered, and Lowder began to plan for making each mission chapel into a parish church. It required only more money, perhaps ten thousand pounds, to buy the church in Wellclose Square and to build a proper church in Wapping. Mackonochie's appointment to St. Alban's, Holborn, in 1862 provided a temporary set-back, but in 1863 two more priests came to Wellclose Square, and by 1866 their number had risen to five. It seemed that the Mission's chronic clergy shortage was finally at an end.

Plans to make St. Saviour's into a genuine parish had been stalled by two factors: difficulties with the Danish government over its purchase, and the 1860 designation of a small chapel on near-by Pell Street as an independent parish (St. Matthew's), thereby drastically reducing the potential size of St. Saviour's district. But plans for building a church in Wapping proceeded with great success. Seven thousand pounds were raised, the foundations were laid in 1865, and the church of St. Peter's was consecrated by the Bishop in June 1866. [19] It was designated an independent parish, with a district of about 8000 people taken from St. George's-in-the-East and St. Paul's, Shadwell, by the end of the year. Lowder, of course, was named Vicar. [20] He and one assistant moved down to Wapping to be in the new parish. The only cloudy issue was the future of St. Saviour's, now tied in a complex way to both St. George's and St. Peter's. It was ironic that the Wapping portion of the Mission should have been permanently established first, because Lowder had originally judged the Wellclose Square area "apparently the most suitable for strictly missionary work." [21] In 1867 Lowder began to plan for the building of a new church that would stand near Wellclose Square in the middle of a potential new parish. Three clergy remained at St. Saviour's, building toward its parochial independence.

But within a year these plans were to crumble. In early 1868, suddenly and without any warning either to Lowder or their own parishioners, all three of the St. Saviour's clergy seceded to the Roman Church. The blow, wrote Robert Linklater, "nearly killed Mr. Lowder." [22] Surely it devastated the Mission. Left with only one curate, Lowder had no alternative but to liquidate the Mission's work in the Wellclose Square district. The church, the mission house, and the associated schools were given up, while those clubs that could not be transferred to Wapping were abandoned. Lowder had become, once again, simply a parish priest. Instead of an annual report, he issued a letter to his supporters, declaring that ". . . we can scarcely retain the name of S. George's Mission for a parochial work," but requesting their continued financial aid. [23] Support for Lowder was not long in coming. Offers of both money and clerical help were frequent. W. J. E. Bennett left his parish in Frome to assist Lowder throughout Lent. Mackonochie denounced the seceders to the S.S.C.: "It remained for three of our younger brethren, with heartless treachery, to do this work of Christ (on which our older brethren had expended. from the very foundation of the Society, so much care and love) a wrong which Protestantism, Prejudice, Sin, and open Ungodliness had failed to effect." [24] But on balance, the effect of the dramatic secessions seems to have been a good one for the Mission. Henceforth Lowder concentrated his energies entirely on a single parish, and henceforth he was far more successful in his attempts to attract stable curates. Lowder never had fewer than three assisting priests. Usually there were four. Robert Linklater came in 1872 and the next year Lincoln Stanhope Wainright arrived, never to leave until his death fifty-six years later. There were to be no more secessions. In 1878, just a decade after the debacle, Lowder could report: "While neighbouring incumbents in the East of London constantly complain that they cannot obtain such assistance, S. Peter's has been privileged to retain a full and most efficient staff for nearly ten years." [25]

The Sisters

But the clergy were only half of the St. Peter's staff. The other half were the sisters of the new Community of the Holy Cross, an order that looked to Lowder as founder. In many ways, however, their real founder was J. M. Neale's sister, who became Mother Elizabeth. The order grew with remarkable speed, from three members in 1857 to twelve just four years later. At first the sisters, like those at Wantage, did not adopt any distinctive dress. They were definitely a missionary order, dedicated to service and works of mercy, particularly the rehabilitation of prostitutes. Their devotional life was focused around the daily eucharist at the Mission chapel and the recitation of the day offices from the English translation of the breviary. Later they would gradually assume monastic garb, and still later they would become an enclosed, contemplative order based on the Benedictine rule. But at their beginning they were fully a part of the parish staff. Every sister was assigned a district of the parish for which she was responsible; each visited from door-to-door within her district, urging the people to receive the sacraments, caring as she could for the ill and the poor. It was not an unprecedented plan. Most urban parishes in the Church of England were far too large to permit the systematic clergy visitations that had, two centuries earlier, formed the ideal for a George Herbert or a Richard Baxter. By the mid-nineteenth century, "district lady visitors" had become an accepted part of Anglican parochial practice. The sisters in Wapping represented simply an anglo-catholic refinement of this practice. It was an effective refinement, partly because Elizabeth Neale proved an effective superior. Lowder wrote of them appreciatively: "The influence of a religious community living amongst the poor, always at hand for any work of mercy, going in and out daily amongst them, their ears always open to their troubles and tales of distress, and their hands stretched out to relieve them to the full extent of their power, and while they minister to their bodies not forgetting to turn their thoughts to the more important concerns of their souls; and all this under the direction and superintendence of the Clergy, has already produced a beneficial effect upon the District. [26]

The formation of a sisterhood was a logical extension of parochial work for many anglo-catholics. But in Lowder's case, it may have owed a debt, also, to Vincent de Paul's 1633 foundation of the Sisters of Charity, the first active apostolate for women since the early church. Vincent had written of his order: "Instead of a convent they have only the dwellings of the sick; for a cell, some poor chamber; . . . for a chapel, the parish church; for a cloister, the streets of a town; for enclosure, obedience; for a gate, the fear of God; for a veil, holy modesty." [27] It was a vision too strikingly like that of Lowder's to be a coincidence. But if Lowder drew his inspiration from an earlier model, he used his order to do something quite new. One great problem faced by any East End clergyman was his association in the popular mind with a relieving officer. Requests for money and other assistance could consume much of a slum priest's time and energies, to say nothing of his resources. Lowder handled the problem very simply: he turned all works of corporeal relief over to the sisters, reserving to himself and his fellow-clergy the "spiritual" care of his parishioners. It was a shrewd and effective decision, for it freed him from the constant burden of what Christian missionaries would later call "rice Christians." There is no reason to believe that this decision was a particularly self-conscious one; probably it merely seemed to Lowder a logical extension of the sisterhood's work. But it represented a dramatic break with the experience of almost every other clergyman in the Victorian East End. In 1863 Lowder wrote:

> The help of the Sisters has been most valuable during the past year in visiting the Poor and Sick, and teaching in the Girls' and Infant School in Calvert Street, which are entirely in their charge. The temporal care of the Poor in this District is also in their hands, so that the Clergy have only the more important and spiritual matters to attend to in their visits and ministrations. We should be very glad to welcome the assistance of more ladies. who would thus dedicate themselves to GOD's service . . . [28]

In a later report, Lowder wrote that charity was dispensed only after careful investigation by the sisters and the clergy to determine the worthiness of the particular claim. [29] But it is obvious that the primary investigation was undertaken by the sisters, and it was they who distributed the food, medicine, and clothing to the poor of Wapping.

The most dramatic of the work involving the sisters, and probably the most important single event in the history of the Wapping Mission, was that engendered by the cholera epidemic that swept through East London from July to September 1866, just a month after the consecration of St. Peter's. The Guardians of the Poor Law Union commandeered the casual wards of the local workhouse for a cholera hospital and summoned the Nursing Sisters of St. John the Divine to take over its administration and care. Lowder and the Mission sisters worked closely with the nurses, caring for the sick as long as they could be kept at home, carrying them to the workhouse when they were judged to endanger their families. Only about fifty of the parishioners who contracted cholera survived. Ignorant of the disease's true cause, Lowder nonetheless blamed the unsanitary conditions of his parish: ". . . it can, I say, be no wonder that when the cholera once broke out amongst us it should have proved most fatal; in fact, that the death-rate, in proportion to the population, should have been higher than in any other part of London." [30] Seemingly, Lowder and the sisters were everywhere, daily visiting the sick both in the hospital and at home, inducing volunteers from the West End to come and aid the parish effort. One sister was always on duty, night and day, to receive calls for medicine or clothing. "In the morning, when the Clergy, after the services in St. Peter's, were going forth to

their daily rounds, while some [sister] would take the pressing or danger-
ous cases which remained from the day before, another would find out
from the relieving officer's list at the workhouse, and the Sisters' list at
the Mission House, the new cases which needed attention." [31]

It was sad work, for the progress of the disease was rapid and
the few medicines available did little to alleviate the suffering. "The sud-
denness of the attack, the awful rapidity with which it spread, the speedy
issue of each seizure, requiring immediate attention both for spiritual and
physical relief, continually baffled our most earnest endeavours to provide
it." [32] Few of the sufferers could receive communion because of their
vomiting, but Lowder or the sisters attempted to be at every death-bed.
Remarkably, not one of the staff contracted the disease. Lowder's own
sister, who came to stay at the Mission in order to help, wrote home in
the middle of August:

> I carry little bottles of camphor and give them where they
> are wanted. We are all very well here, and everybody very
> busy, but we are not at all a melancholy party, everybody
> in good spirits. I generally see Charles some time every
> day, and he is quite well. [33]

Lowder appealed for money and clothing in a letter to the **Times,** the response to which proved overwhelming. A thousand pounds was received
in the first week alone, and an equal amount came in over the next few
months. With such resources, Lowder was enabled to open a public
kitchen that offered food to the destitute and to rent a convalescent home
at Seaford for parishioners who had survived the disease. At the end of
the year, when the epidemic had passed, he wrote: "This generous response, besides large gifts of wine, brandy, clothes, &c., enabled the
Clergy and Sisters to meet the wants which pressed upon them with all
necessary relief." [34] At Lowder's request, the Bishop and his wife came
into the parish immediately after the epidemic had peaked. Tait visited
the cholera wards, met with the sisters, and led a congregation of 900 in
the litany and prayers for the sick. It proved to be a turning point in the
history of the parish.

The cholera epidemic broke down the lingering hostility toward the Mission staff. Lowder wrote of the new "trust" and "respect" he
felt; ". . . there can be no doubt that the effect of this mournful visitation was largely to increase the influence of the Clergy and Sisters for

good in the Mission districts. Many doors were eagerly opened to them in the time of danger which had never been opened before." [35] From the time of the epidemic until his death, he was universally called "Father Lowder" within the parish. [36] Just as importantly, the epidemic seems to have warmed relations between Lowder and his determinedly protestant bishop. Henceforth, Tait and his successors never inhibited any of the Mission clergy. Finally, the epidemic also spurred the public acceptance of sisterhoods. Seven different orders had sent nurses to the East End in the summer of 1866, and their work had earned for them a general admiration. Trench recorded the words of one sister who had been at St. Peter's since 1860; "We had never any trouble after the cholera." [37]

Until the time of the epidemic, much of the Mission's day-to-day ministry was necessarily carried on by the sisters. It was they who did the regular visiting, calling on Lowder only in cases of illness or spiritual need. It was they who provided the food, clothing, and other works of relief. Lowder's own staff was too small and his concerns too many for him to do all the work of a parish priest. And he did not intend to be just a parish clergyman. He considered himself a mission priest, the head of a religious order that was called to forge a new pattern of slum ministry. But after the mid-sixties the reality, if not Lowder's own view, changed. His sisterhood veered toward a less missionary and more contemplative life; fewer and fewer of the sisters remained in the Mission House attached to the parish. Finally, in 1869 the order began a move to a new "mother house" at Walworth: it was a step away from the active apostolate and toward enclosure. Fortunately, by this time Lowder's staff had finally stabilized. While sisters continued to work in the parish, Lowder and his curates took over progressively more of the parochial ministry. Trench recognized this when she wrote, "His work seems, as it went on, to have become more concentrated and entirely parochial, partly from the want of funds to enable him to branch out in other directions." [38] In 1876, when he was elected Master of the S.S.C., he turned down the offer, pleading his parochial obligations. It might amuse him that he is today remembered primarily as a model parish priest.

St. Peter's, London Docks

Besides his ministry to individuals, Lowder also developed a variety of clubs, institutions, and associations that made St. Peter's one of the most highly organized parishes in the East End. By far the most important of these were the schools. Repeatedly he argued that every city parish must maintain its own school system, in order to combat "the insufficiency of the so-called religious instruction in Board [state] schools." [39] The teaching at the Mission schools did not share this lack. From the beginning the clergy took classes in Christian dogma every morning, the children were catechised weekly at the chapel, and all the pupils were expected to attend church on Sundays and festivals. Later there would be a Thursday morning eucharist for the children, as well. Lowder, like almost every other active East End clergyman until the end of the century, saw the children as the church's principal hope for the future. To this end, he founded three schools within the Mission's first year: one for boys, one for girls, and one for infants, all in Wapping. A layman ran the first, while the remaining two were staffed by the sisters. The next year a coeducational school was opened in Wellclose Square, and by 1860 it had attracted enough pupils to split into three different schools along the lines of those in Wapping. Enrollment rose quickly, from fewer than 200 the first year to 540 in 1859 to slightly over 600 in the early sixties, a figure that remained constant until long after Lowder's death. He never seemed to have any difficulty in recruiting teachers; the problem was one of adequate facilities. Writing in 1861, the government inspector reported; "This is the first time of inspection; the children are all of a very poor class, and are very fairly instructed. New premises, however ought to be provided, or at all events, considerable alterations ought to be made in the present room." [40] The abandonment of the Wellclose Square mission in 1868 allowed Lowder to focus on the three schools in Wapping. In 1872 a large building was constructed, and the schools moved into their first suitable facility, their home to the present day.

Despite his reserved personality, Lowder was apparently a popular figure among the children. Numerous accounts recall his customary progress through the streets of Wapping. slowed by a dozen children hiding underneath his cloak or tugging at the hem of his cassock. He did not often teach in the schools, leaving that task to his curates, but he always insisted on taking the church catechisings himself. And he seemed to revel in the schools' annual August outing, for he usually recounted it with a note of real pleasure in his annual report. That for 1864 is typical: "The School treat in August passed off very successfully, the children with a few adult members of the congregation were conveyed in 16 vans to Richmond Park, and the weather being favourable, a very happy day was spent by those who have so few opportunities of enjoying the country air." [41]

The first attempt to organize any parallel institution for adults was made in 1860. Interestingly, the impetus came not from the Mission itself but from an unnamed layman, who--to judge by his friends-- was a broad churchman rather than an anglo-catholic. A house was rented inWellclose Square, the founder moved in, and the Working Man's Institute was formally opened in October. F. D. Maurice gave the inaugural lecture, and he was followed in the succeeding weeks by J. M. Ludlow, Thomas Hughes, and A. P. Stanley, the most noted broad churchmen of their time. Only Charles Kingsley, that movement's novelist, was missing. The Institute attempted at once to be a school and a social club. Besides regular lectures, it provided reading rooms, a circulating library, game rooms, a smoking room that served coffee, and separate facilities for boys. Classes were organized in the basic skills of reading and arithmetic, while French and drawing were also taught. Within a month it had attracted 180 members, a number that grew to 400 by the end of the first year. Lowder showed great reticence about the new Institute, probably because of its theological bias, but he did see in the men's response a rejection of the St. George's rioters: "The existence and success of the Institute has plainly proved how little the real working men of the parish sympathized with the abettors of the disturbance in the Parish Church . . . ." [42] By the time the Wellclose Square mission had closed, the Institute had moved to Gravel Lane, where it diverged somewhat from its original purpose and became "rather a dining than a literary club." [43]

The associations Lowder himself founded were all devotional "confraternities" that aimed to unite the Mission's communicants around the eucharist and a rule of life. They stemmed from two unnamed societies begun in 1862, one "in honour of the Blessed Sacrament of our Lord's Body and Blood, at which special instruction is given to the communicants," and one "in which each member promises to pray every day for the conversion of sinners, especially for those around them." [44] During the next year these were merged into a general "Confraternity of communicants" in union with the new, national organization for lay anglo-catholics, the Confraternity of the Blessed Sacrament. By 1871, however, this single guild had divided again along lines of sex and age: "There are about 100 members in the Confraternities of S. Peter [for men] and the Good Shepherd [for women], which are for adult communicants, and about sixty in the Guilds of the Holy Child [for boys] and S.

Katherine [for girls], which are for younger members." [45] The adult
confraternities shared much the same rules: members should attend the
eucharist on Sundays and other festivals, should communicate at least
once a month, and should pray for the Mission staff, the conversion of
sinners, and the re-unification of the church. The guilds for children had
simpler rules focusing on moral purity. But each of the guilds had a practical aspect, as well. The dues accumulated by St. Katharine's Guild
might be used to help in the marriage settlement for any poor member.
And Lowder made one scant reference to an activity that grew out of the
Guild of the Holy Child: the members ". . .also meet in their club,
which is open in the evening for games, reading, &c." [46] It is notable
that Lowder never founded any club or society purely for the physical betterment or the social pleasure of his parishioners. He was a man of the
altar and the confessional. In this he stands out very clearly from his
contemporary East End clergymen, even from other anglo-catholics.
Lowder thought of himself only as a priest. The Mission had sisters and
lay assistants to see to his people's "unspiritual" needs.

    These assistants did not entirely share Lowder's reluctance to
trespass on the merely social sphere. In the annual reports there are allu-
sions to a variety of organizations in the Wellclose Square district: a fife
and drum band, a shoe club, a clothing fund, and a penny bank. After
1869, probably because St. Peter's then had a stable body of curates, the
annual reports reveal a series of new organizations in the Wapping district as well: a burial guild (1869), a local branch of the English Church
Union (1871), a Destitute Children's Dinner Society (1871), a coopera-
tive kitchen (1872), a hostel for the aged (1872), a branch of the Church
of England Temperance Society (1876), and a branch of the Church of
England Working Men's Society (1876). The two "dinner societies" attempted to provide healthful meals, at least during the winter months, to
those who could not otherwise afford them. Admittance was by a small
payment or a certificate from one of the Mission staff. Similarly, the co-
operative kitchen represented an attempt by working men and their wives
to band together in order to provide themselves more economical meals.
But still, except for Lowder's one allusion to the boys' club, there is no
record of any purely recreational association, no reference to any social
club that provided an alternative to the public house.

    After Lowder's death this changed, perhaps under Wainright's
prodding. "The Annual Report for 1885" lists twenty-five "parochial organizations," including all the associations of Lowder's time, but adding

a lending library, a loan society, and eight new recreational clubs. Perhaps Lowder felt uneasy about the proliferation of societies after 1869. If
so, he would have had good reason, for later East End clergymen would
find themselves and their parochial work almost lost in a maze of associations. Whether from this or another concern, Lowder borrowed an idea
from St. Michael's, Shoreditch. In 1874 he founded a St. Peter's Church
Society, consisting of the combined membership of all the various organizations, "to unite all our confraternities and guilds, whether of adults
or young people, in one general Society, . . .as a bond of union between
Communicants." [47] The Society did not last after Lowder's death, but
while he lived he saw it as a sort of vestry: "The Clergy have an opportunity of learning the minds of their people in Parochial Council, and addressing them on matters of common interest." [48] In a way, it was a
brave step for a priest who was more inclined to clerical direction than to
any conciliar notion of authority.

There was one part of St. Peter's work that diverged sharply
from this general pattern. St. Agatha's Mission, founded by Robert Linklater at the eastern (Shadwell) end of the parish in 1869, proved to have a
rather different character from the rest of the parochial efforts. There was
no opposition from Lowder; he welcomed Linklater as a part-time assistant in 1869 and then as a full-time curate three years later. Linklater obviously idolized the older priest, as is evident from the several long accounts he contributed to the Trench biography. But he was a very
different man from Lowder, with a less reserved and more audacious manner. And he created a very different sort of ministry in St. Agatha's. [49]
The new Mission began with a night school to provide working men
with the educational rudiments most of them had missed; soon one hundred were coming three nights a week. Linklater aimed his Mission at the
poorest of the young working men, the "surging mob of noisy and blas-
pheming roughs," as he called the members of his bible class, which met
twice a week. As a result he faced some curious difficulties, as on the
night when the police broke into his classroom and seized one of his pupils. But Linklater obviously enjoyed the rough give-and-take. He moved
on to found a free day school for very young children, a drum and fife
band, and various clubs for both girls and boys. Later, once his work had
become established, he began short "missionary services" consisting of
hymns, prayers, and a brief sermon. But at St. Agatha's, unlike St. Peter's, there was never any necessary connection between club membership
and church attendance. Linklater thought of his work as specifically

"missionary" and spoke of the necessity of "raising the masses" as a precondition to "christianising" them. After Lowder's death and Linklater's
subsequent departure, St. Agatha's gradually withered as a separate Mission. Increasingly the parish took over the remaining school and clubs
as part of its own work.

By that time St. Peter's had one of the most crowded service
schedules of any church in London.
Three years before his death Lowder wrote:

> There has been always one, and for many years there have
> been two celebrations of the Holy Eucharist daily in S.
> Peter's. The first is at 6.45, the second at 8 a.m., with
> Matins at 7.30. Choral Evensong is at 8 p.m. with, on
> Fridays and eves of Festivals, a sermon. A Communicant
> Class is held on Thursday evenings, and during a portion
> of the year a Confirmation Class Tuesdays. On Sundays
> we have Celebrations at 7, 8, and 9 a.m.; Matins at
> 10.30; : High Celebration and sermon at 11.15, except
> on Festivals, when Matins is at 10.15, and there is a pro-
> cession before the High Celebration. Litany is said at
> 2.30, the children's service at 3.30, and evensong at 7
> p.m. During Advent the *Dies Irae* and during Lent the
> *Miserere* is sung, and an instruction is given after Even-
> song; at other times there is a Bible Class. On week-
> days, during Advent and Lent, there is a meditation in
> Church on Mondays; a Mission service, consisting of a
> metrical litany, hymns, and sermon, on Wednesdays; and
> the Stations of the Cross on Fridays. Confessions are
> heard on Fridays and Saturdays, and on special days before
> Great Festivals. [50]

In addition, Lowder preached occasional outdoor sermons, hosted parish
missions led by fellow S.S.C. members every two or three years, and observed the traditional solemnities of Holy Week prescribed by the Roman
Missal. Beginning with Good Friday 1869, Lowder even took the stations of the cross outdoors in a procession throughout Wapping, preaching at each of the fourteen stations himself. It was a regimen to daunt
the most catholic of priests. Remembering that his personal rule required
further time every day for meditation and study, the wonder is that Lowder ever left his church at all. Yet he was an earnest, if formidable, pas-

tor, and the numbers he attracted to his church reflected that commitment.

When Lowder first went to Wapping, only three communicants of St. George's lived in the district. During the next twenty years Lowder and his assistants baptized an average of 120 people annually, presented about fifty every year for confirmation, and brought the communicants on the parish roll up to about 300. [51] When Lowder came to Wapping in 1856 he was entering an essentially unchurched area, one of the poortst districts in all London. When he died just under a quarter century later, he left behind a flourishing church, large congregations, and a sizable roll of well-instructed communicants. It was a considerable accomplishment, made even uore impressive by the lack of any residuum of lapsed churchmen whose loyalty to the Church of England he could hope to enliven. Almost every one of Lowder's communicants was a convert to the church; a great many, perhaps the majority, were baptized by Lowder himself. Lowder made the point over and over, presumably in response to supporters who felt that his work was not showing sufficient results: "If we had made it our chief object to obtain great and conspicuous results as the very object of our work, we might have chosen other districts of the metropolis where the ground had been better prepared or at least where the character of the population afforded a better prospect of large and respectable congregations." [52]

Yet he need not have been defensive. The speed of the Mission's early growth was remarkable. By 1861, only five years after it was begun, the Mission had a congregation almost half the size it was to achieve twenty years later. Several indices demonstrate this. The 1859 annual report said that more than 500 had been baptized to date and that almost 200 were regular attendants at the Mission chapels. By 1861 the communicant list had risen to 150, and by the next year twenty more had been added. Despite the instability of many of its early clergy, despite the temporary nature of its chapels, the Mission could claim a larger congregation than that in most East End churches.

What is perhaps even more striking is that there was no decline in attendance after Lowder's death. In 1884, according to the annual report, 450 made their Easter communions and the communicant roll numbered more than 500.

Toward the end of his life Lowder was usually ill and frequently away recuperating in the country, but when in Wapping, he would permit no diminution of the usual schedule. It was an arduous one. Link-

later has left a long account of a typical Sunday for the clergy; it ran
from 7 a.m. to well past 10 p.m. with less than an hour for rest. [53]
Life at the clergy house was not an idle one. The St. Peter's clergy spent
much of their time in church, celebrating the sacrament Lowder custo-
marily called "the Holy Sacrifice," reading the offices, hearing confessions. The last was especially important, for Lowder always maintained
that, "The hearing of Confessions is the very backbone and marrow of
pastoral work." Yet the clergy were also out among their people every
day. Though the distance between clergy and laity was great, the staff at
St. Peter's probably knew their parishioncrs as well as any clergy in the
East End. None served them any better.

Lowder died in September 1880 while in Austria, where he had
gone in one of his many attempts to regain his health. His body was returned to St. Peter's, where twelve successive requiem eucharists were
celebrated, including ones by Bryan King, Mackonochie, Linklater, and
Wainright. More than a thousand, two hundred of whom were clergy,
followed the funeral train to Chislehurst, where Lowder's body was finally buried. The next Sunday Harry Jones, the broad-church Rector of St.
George's-in-the-East, preached a memorial sermon:

> I need not say that he was loved by the poor amongst
> whom he ministered, and with whom, however ignorant
> they may have been of mere ecclesiastical nomenclature
> he was "Father" Lowder--always ready to visit them in
> their affliction, and help them according to his ability, to
> be unspotted in the world. They mourn for him with a
> sorrow which is deeply sincere, for they well know what
> a loving and unsparing friend they have lost in losing
> him. [54]

It was one of the largest funerals for a parish priest in Victorian England. It would be surpassed at St. Peter's only forty-nine years later, and
then only by the funeral for Wainwright.

Perhaps because ill health had kept him away from the parish
so often during his later years, Lowder's death hardly affected the growth
of St. Peter's. But that fact is also a testimony to the strength of his religious teaching. No other East End parish of the nineteenth or twentieth
centuries has survived the loss of a charismatic pastor with so little diminution. From the time Wainright became vicar in early 1884, the future

of the parish was assured. Wainright was a curious, unprepossessing
man. When Mackonochie had became Vicar in 1882, he was horrified to
discover that his senior curate had not taken a holiday in ten years. He ordered Wainright away for a month's vacation. Two days later a parishioner encountered the errant curate walking back along Gravel Lane:

> "Why, Father!" young Cairncross exclaimed, "I thought
> you had gone away for a month."
> "Yes!" Father Wainright answered, "but I couldn't breathe
> the horrid air. And they didn't seem to have any fleas, so
> I had to get back to this lovely air." [55]

Wainright never again attempted a holiday, and rarely was he away from
the parish even overnight. A small, rather bumbling, effervescent man,
he had attracted--by the time of the 1902-03 **Daily News** census--one
of the East End's largest congregations. Wainright earned an exceptional
two paragraphs in Booth's study:

> In the adjoining parish of St. Peter's, we find one of the
> most concentrated and distinctive pieces of parochial work
> that London has to show. The devotion of the vicar is
> absolute, and his spirit dominates everything, making the
> whole work focus in the realization, so far as it can be re-
> alized, of the High Church ideal of a parish of devout
> cummunicants. . . . There is an almost complete circle of
> parish organizations, schools, guilds and clubs; some-
> thing for those of every age and both sexes. . . . The
> treats and charities are on a lavish scale. . . . But it is the
> individual soul that is his especial care. His mind and
> heart are filled with solicitude for the salvation of his peo-
> ple. . . . The value of it is difficult to measure. Religion,
> to gain strength, is lowered to superstition; other church-
> es are robbed, but still the bulk of the population are un-
> touched; the devotion to the poor is complete, but it is to
> be feared that they can hardly escape pauperization. In
> these matters we require to attach many different mean-
> ings to the word success. [56]

Booth was unfair in characterizing religion at St. Peter's as intentionally
superstitious. Few parishes anywhere made a greater attempt to teach orthodox doctrine to average parishioners. Booth may have been unfair in

charging St. Peter's with robbing other churches and with pauperizing the already poor. Wainright never set out to attract those who were not genuinely his parishioners, and his catholic notion of charity at least arose from genuine religious impulses. But in a larger sense Booth did raise the real question to be asked of St. Peter's or any other slum parish: to what extent did it affect the bulk of the population? At no time in its history did St. Peter's attract more than ten percent of Wapping's population, and even then most of its congregation consisted of children. Today much of Wapping is forlorn. No longer a slum like much of Whitechapel, it nonetheless lacks Whitechapel's life and ethnic brassiness. More largely destroyed by German bombs than by social planners, its former slum tenements have been replaced by row upon row of monotonous Council housing. St. Peter's stands woefully empty, a hollow monument to its long-dead saints. Perhaps the majority of the parishioners are second, third, even fourth generation residents of the district. But few of the residents seem to socialize outside the five public houses. Wapping is a quiet, sad place, only a mile from the City and yet so far from the rest of London that a temporary American resident can become a focus of community interest for months. Today one looks in vain for the long-range effect of a Lowder or a Wainright.

Lowder: An Assessment

Historians have often noted the movement of young, anglo-catholic clergy into England's slums, full of confidence that their Tractarian theology, their incipient ritualism, and their commitment to celibacy would be vindicated by their labors among the most peripheral of British humanities. They were drawn to the slums by a combination of attractions: the romantic pull of missionary service within their own land, their quasi-monastic desire for heroic self-sacrifice, the possibility of establishing a mission among people wholly uncorrupted by middle-class commitments to the existing Church of England. These attractions were only buttressed by their lack of employment possibilities elsewhere; there were far more anglo-catholic curates than there were parishes ready to receive them.

Yet this movement lacked the monolithic character usually claimed for it. At least in the East End, only a minority of the parishes became anglo-catholic during the Victorian era, and of these, only St.

George's Mission shared the features often assigned to the movement as a whole. That this movement did not bear out its early hopes is equally clear. Of all the anglo-catholic parishes in the East End, St. Peter's London Docks, was one of the very few that attracted huge congregations by the century's end. Yet to read the anglo-catholic literature for the generation after 1850 is to become acquainted with a movement of historic proportions, with dozens of young priests going down to the slums, with hopes for the conversion of the entire industrial proletariat, with the conviction that "high" ceremonial and "definite" church principles would prove their worth there as nowhere else. Despite the caveats of the **Daily News** census, most historians of the Church of England have accepted that picture of the movement as reality. But was there, after all, such a movement, or was it, rather, the product of a Victorian myth?

Despite the movement's presumed focus on London's dockland this question cannot be answered with certainty from an analysis of East End parishes alone. Perhaps it cannot be answered at all, for that would require a knowledge of England's slum parishes that may lie beyond the reach of modern historians. Few of these parishes kept any adequate records, and of that small number, fewer still possess archives that have survived both later disinterest and the Second World War's destruction. Little remains, for example, of the model anglo-catholic parish, St. Augustine's, Whitechapel, consecrated in 1879 and gutted in the war just over sixty years later. This chapter has focused on St. George's Mission not only because it was the most important anglo-catholic experiment in East London, but also because dedicated parishioners have preserved nearly every scrap of paper and every recollection from their church's early years.

The data that remains, however, is sufficient to cast doubt on the reality of a mass migration of anglo-catholics into the slums. The usual view of that movement, both in the Victorian and later periods, seems to have been derived from two very atypical parishes: St. Albans, Holborn, and St. Peter's, London Docks. Historical imagination has fused the two, and out of that fusion has been created a romantic picture of numerous young anglo-catholic clergy, banded together in semi-monastic "colleges," laboring mightily for their version of the Christian faith among the dockers and other casual workers.

Yet this movement into the slums, even if its reality is not confirmed by the evidence, has a life of its own. It is not an invention of twentieth-century historians, for it was widespread by at least the mid-eighteen-sixties. It was, whether true or not, a part of the Victorian mythology, a part that helped form two generations of anglo-catholic clergy. In a weakened sense the myth is still alive, still inspiring the labors of a few young clergymen. For that, their parishioners may be grateful.

To a considerable extent, anglo-catholicism was vindicated in the public mind by the labors of its slum priests, particularly Charles Lowder. But their work had another, deleterious effect, one only dimly perceived by their protestant opponents. They introduced an unprecedented degree of congregationalism into the Church of England. The **Tourist's Church Guide** was symptomatic. Ostensibly published for the aid of travellers, it was no Baedeker to lead itinerating Englishmen through medieval churches and great cathedrals. It was, instead, a handbook to guide ordinary churchmen away from their local parishes to churches with "advanced" ritual. The rapid subdivision of historic parishes early in the nineteenth century, together with the later opposition of evangelicals to any liturgical innovations, only contributed to this change. There is a profound irony here. The anglo-catholics gained respectability through their heroic parish efforts. Yet those very efforts served to weaken the Church of England's parochial system. To an extent the Establishment rested on that very system and to that same extent the anglo-catholics worked to undermine the Establishment. It was no accident that by the century's end, many high churchmen had become vehement opponents of a state-controlled church. The Establishment, in fact if not in law, may have been lost in the Victorian era.

For Lowder himself, that irony had a very personal dimension. He never intended to be merely a parish priest. Rather, he felt called to the "home mission" field, to found an order like the Vincentians, to pioneer new ways of ministry in the slums. Yet he failed in all those intentions. Only toward the end of his life did he manage to collect around him a stable body of curates, and by that time he was too sick and too burdened with parochial responsibilities to superintend a religious order. Originally a missionary effort of the S.S.C., St. George's Mission rapidly became Lowder's own effort. Every attempt to reach beyond his district gradually faded from his grasp. Unwittingly and against his every instinct, Lowder became merely a parish priest, one of the greatest parish priests in the Victorian era.

Lowder's success is surprising, for he lacked the warm and easy personality such work usually demands. Shy, rigid, intensely clerical, he seemed better suited to the monastery than to the parish. He was an authoritarian figure, never allowing his parishioners to approach him as an equal, relaxing his habitual reserve only in the presence of children. Yet he possessed a hidden talent for administration. By the end of its second year, the Mission had very nearly assumed its final form. Only two years later the Mission's schools had nearly reached their maximum enrollment. The cholera epidemic of 1866 marked a turning point. With his enormous capacity for work, Lowder organized his whole district to meet the needs of the survivors while caring for the sick and the dying. "Father Lowder," as he then became, finally earned the love as well as the loyalty of his people. He attributed his success to his ritualism and to his teaching of church principles. But his achievements owed far more to the character of the man himself.

III

THE BROAD CHURCHMEN

There were not many broad churchmen in the East End, and two of them shared the same name. Samuel Augustus Barnett, later Canon of Bristol and then of Westminster, worked in Whitechapel for more than thirty years alongside his wife, Henrietta Rowland, later Dame Henrietta, Commander of the British Empire. By the end of the nineteenth century, Barnett was the best-known of all East London clergymen. At least four other East End incumbents shared his theological views. Brooke Lambert, the Vicar of St. Mark's, Whitechapel, from 1866 to 1870, had shed his earlier evangelicalism while a student of F. D. Maurice at King's College. But Lambert's health broke down, and except for one year as Barnett's curate-in-charge he was never to return to the East End. John Richard Green, the noted historian, became vicar of St. Philip's, Stepney Way, in 1866. But his health broke down, also. Using his repeated periods of convalescence for scholarship, he was remembered after his death as a writer and a founder of the Oxford Historical Society, rather than as a parish clergyman. Septimus Hansard, another former colleague of Maurice, served during the same period as the faithful and uncontroversial Rector of St. Matthew's, Bethnal Green. More important was Harry Jones, who became Rector of St. George's-in-the-East in 1873 and was a close friend of the Barnetts. Jones, however, was not known for parochial zeal. An interested observer of London life, he attracted only a small congregation and failed to make a great impact on his parish. The Barnetts were left almost alone to represent missionary broad churchmanship in the East End.

In March of 1873 Barnett, then just thirty years old, accepted the living of St. Jude's, Whitechapel. It was as curious an offer as an acceptance. The Bishop's letter had hardly been encouraging: ". . . it is the worst parish in my diocese, inhabited mainly by a criminal population, and one which has, I fear, been much corrupted by doles." [1] On the oth-

er hand, little in Barnett's overly protected background as the eldest son of
a rigidly Tory merchant had prepared him for the move. His three years
of reading law and history at Wadham College, Oxford, had hardly
changed his inherited conservatism. And at the time of the Bishop's offer
he was engaged to a young and brilliant woman who seemed to regard her
impending marriage more as a religious duty than a romantic commitment. Spare, prematurely balding, rather sickly, not blessed with great
intellect or force of character or eloquent speech, Barnett was an unprepossessing man, hardly one destined to become a leading figure in the
East End. Yet, by the time of his resignation in 1892 Barnett had developed a unique ministry in East London, had founded the first settlement
house, and had done much to revolutionize the pattern of contemporary
social work. A recent article by Leonard Cowie has argued that the Barnetts, rather than Sydney and Beatrice Webb, might be considered the
founders of the modern welfare state. [2] After a visit to England, during
which he had spent some time with Barnett, the French statesman Clémenceau remarked, "I have met three really great men in England, and
one was a little pale clergyman in Whitechapel. " [3]

Barnett's dedication to slum work had long roots. While still
"a very young man" according to his wife, he had written a statement of
faith that he afterwards kept in his desk drawer:

> I think of what is my object in life. I see it must be to
> do good, to improve the condition of the people. Before
> attempting this, I ought to consider how far their condi-
> tion falls short of what it might be. I ought to see where
> the poor suffer, how far these sufferings are due to bad
> laws and might be affected by good laws, or whether they
> might have what is best in life if they could simply be
> good. [4]

From this early intimation that the cure to poverty might lie in both personal goodness and changes in the law Barnett was never to deviate.

After taking second-class honors in law and history at Oxford,
Barnett spent two years teaching at Winchester College in order to save
enough money to fulfill another early dream, a trip to America. Since no
letters or journals from the period survive, his motivations are not clear.
But given his faith in the inevitability of progress and his continuing dis-
content with the rigidities of the British class structure, he may well have

viewed America as a model of the future society. Twenty-five years later, after a subsequent journey to the United States, he would write: "Man left to himself has endless resources. This is the contribution given by America to the traveller's estimate of human nature, and it calls him to trust all men more, to give to the poorest more responsibility and less relief." [5] In any case, his 1867 trip--during which he visited every major city between Boston and New Orleans--was not entirely sanguine. He felt keenly the tensions left in the wake of the War between the States. And he left one, rather cryptic, comment on the experience: "Born and nurtured in an atmosphere of Toryism, what I saw and heard there knocked all the Toryism out of me." [6]

From his youth Barnett had intended to take orders, but of his reasons or of the early religious influences upon him he left little record. He had been sent to Wadham by his father because of the rigid Tory politics and the evangelical piety of its warden, but the resulting collegiate atmosphere did not prove congenial to the younger Barnett. His wife remembers his saying later that he "greatly disliked the undergraduates' prayer-meetings, feeling that it was neither healthy nor modest to examine other people's souls nor to expose his own." [7] Apparently no one man had exerted any great religious influence upon him until 1867, when he went to serve his first curacy under W. H. Fremantle, Rector of St. Mary's, Bryanston Square, in the London district of Marylebone. Later the Dean of Ripon, Fremantle was a disciple of F. D. Maurice and, together with Llewelyn Davies, one of London's two most noted broad churchmen. Working at St. Mary's for five years, preaching once a fortnight and teaching in the parish schools, Barnett read widely and absorbed much of his Rector's Maurician theology. Fremantle wrote of him at this time: "He was always liberal in thought and act, his heart was with the poor, and he sought their good, but his larger activities which made him famous were at most in an inchoate condition." Yet indications of his future work were already present. He had chosen to live in the poorest section of his largely well-to-do parish, and his principal enthusiasms were a clubroom he ran for workingmen and the reform of poor relief. A colleague at this time, A. S. W. Young, remembered that Barnett's mind always ran to sociology rather than to theology. [8]

It was at St. Mary's that Barnett was introduced into a remarkable collection of women--including Octavia Hill, Beatrice Webb, and Henrietta Rowland, his future wife--all of whom worked among the poor of the East End. Beatrice Webb has left her first impressions of Barnett:

". . . a diminutive body clothed in shabby and badly assorted garments, big knobby and prematurely bald head, small black eyes set close together, sallow complexion and a thin and patchy pretence of a beard, Barnett, at first sight, was not pleasing to contemplate! . . . [Yet he had] an utter absence of personal vanity, an almost exaggerated christian humility . . ." [9] Throughout his life Barnett had the ability to attract and hold the loyalty of a legion of women co-workers. From them he learned much of his attitude toward poor relief, or what today would be called social work. To them he gave unstinting admiration and faith in their capacities. Later in life he was to claim for himself merely that he had the courage of his wife's convictions.

Barnett constantly decried all restrictions on the role of women in society. At St. Jude's in 1874 he founded a parish school to teach boys and girls together, for "When girls are taught with boys, they will learn much from which they are shut out in 'girls' schools; they will learn also to respect themselves; the boys, too, meeting girls as equals and competitors, will cease to scorn and tease them while they will themselves learn to be much more quiet and gentle." [10] Parochial opposition forced the abandonment of co-education a year later, but Barnett never faltered in his support for women's rights, even suggesting that ordination should be opened to them.

Because they remained childless, Barnett's wife was always able to share his work with a remarkable completeness. One of the obituaries after Samuel Barnett's death in 1913 alluded to this partnership: "Canon and Mrs. Barnett has become, as it were, a single term for one great ideal of life: their work, even if different details can be traced to one or the other of them, was always indivisible and unbrokenly interdependent." [11]

Charity Oganization Society

Victorian philanthropy had been largely administered by women and older men. Thus it was unusual when in 1869, Fremantle and a young Barnett joined Octavia Hill and Henrietta Rowland to found the Charity Organization Society. The scheme grew out of their joint dissatisfaction with the indiscriminate forms of poor relief then so common in London. The various Mansion House Funds, hastily gathered and distributed in times of great privation, were in their view a particular evil. But so, too, was the out-relief practiced constantly by wealthy West End parishes, philanthropic societies, and the Boards of Guardians administering the Poor Law. Individual almsgiving was still extolled as a Christian virtue and practiced by many others of no discernable religious commitment. Frequent small gifts of money to the importuning poor doubtless eased privation, but they did little to reform the underlying causes of poverty: casual labor, unemployment, poorly paid piece-work, and bad housing. However, the focus of the C.O.S. (as it was always called) was different. The new organization concentrated not on the reform of social structures but on the reform of individuals, arguing that the development of good habits--thrift, industry, sobriety--would go far toward eliminating contemporary poverty. The C.O.S. attempted to establish in each Poor Law district of London a committee to screen applicants for relief and to co-ordinate the efforts of the many charitable agencies. Ultimately, the Society hoped, all relief work would be channelled through its various local committees.

Over the next forty years the principles of the C.O.S. largely triumphed in the world of English charity. By 1926 Beatrice Webb could write: "Among the social changes in my lifetime, in the London that I have known, none is more striking than the passing out of the picture of personal almsgiving." [12] The C.O.S. had replaced indiscriminate charity with systematic, "scientific" relief based on detailed investigation of each applicant, attempting to ensure that any aid--when given--should be sufficient not merely to meet an immediate crisis, but to correct the underlying problems of the applicant's situation. Yet even from the beginning there were indications that these principles, when put into practice, could be less than uplifting. At a meeting of the first C.O.S. committee, while Octavia Hill was explaining to a woman why she would not be aided, an older gentleman slipped the applicant a sixpence. The ever-vigilant Samuel Barnett immediately called the offending benefactor to account, and the latter "melted into tears for his own delinquency." [13] Very shortly the C.O.S. would attract criticism for the dogmatic fashion in which it implemented its own principles and for its, suspicious, almost prosecutorial investigation of applicants.

The C.O.S. was at fault for seeing poverty as an individual condition, for failing to understand the social causes of deprivation. Yet the Barnetts, in large measure, remained faithful to the original C.O.S. principles throughout their lives. Shortly after coming to St. Jude's as Vicar, Barnett wrote:

> Indiscriminate charity is among the curses of London. To
> put the result of our observation in the strongest form, I
> would say that "the poor starve because of the alms they
> receive." . . . The people never learn to work or to save,
> out-relief from the [Mansion] House, or the dole of the
> charitable, has stood in the way of providence, which God
> their Father would have taught them. [14]

To correct the abuse of out-relief, Barnett became a Guardian of his Poor
Law Union and established a C.O.S. committee in his new parish, insist-
ing that all applications for funds be channeled through it. But this did
not end the begging, since for some years previously a West End parish
had distributed an annual 500 pounds through St. Jude's. Barnett was
forced to cut a secret door between the vicarage and the church so that he
might escape to summon police help when his home was besieged by
those seeking doles.

The winters of the early eighteen-eighties were particularly
hard ones in East London. Henrietta Barnett confessed that she would
then have often jettisoned her principles in order to bring some small
happiness to the imploring poor, but that her husband stood firm. Relief
was given, but it was a relief consonant with C.O.S. doctrine. Families
of unemployed men were offered support if the men would enter the
workhouse. Pensions were provided for the elderly and the sick. And various forms of low-paid work were invented, from street cleaning to house
repair, to give the unemployed an alternative to the workhouse.

It was not that Barnett was hard-hearted, for he was to accomplish more to the permanent benefit of the East End poor than anyone
else of his generation. It was not that he was ignorant of the social causes of poverty, for he was later to embrace a limited socialism. Barnett
was simply dogmatic. In his 1890 parish report he wrote, "In summing
up the year's thoughts about the poor, the conclusion remains that the
only adequate relief is that which raises character . . . . The poor are not
poor only because the rich are selfish. The poor are as often poor because
of their own want of character." [15] Barnett constantly appealed for patience in dealing with the poor, for working to alleviate the causes and
not merely the symptoms of poverty. These causes, in his view, could
only be corrected by friendship between the classes, by the example and
the sympathy that the middle-class could provide for the poor. "Relief, if

it is to be helpful", he argued, "must follow and not prevent friendship, it must have for its object the good and not the comfort of individuals." [16]

As Barnett matured he became somewhat less opposed to state relief, more open to socialism, and progressively further removed from the C.O.S. He came gradually to understand that the alleviation of poverty required much more than the reformation of individuals. In an 1893 letter he said to his wife: "The East End was despair-creating this morning as I walked to Bethnal Green. I wished you had been with me to help me think. The sight drove me to Socialistic remedies. How can the people rise, crushed in such tombs of streets foul with death?" But his disenchantment with the C.O.S. had begun much earlier. In 1880 he had argued that the C.O.S. must be careful not to disaffect the "kind-hearted", who might break away from a society that substituted "a relief-giving machine" for true charity. [17] By 1886 the break had become public, and the Barnetts withdrew progressively from the C.O.S. central organization, though they remained affiliated with the local committee.

Early Years at St. Jude's

When Samuel Barnett went to Whitechapel in 1873 he was fulfilling an ideal held by his new wife. Though constantly opposed by her family, she had determined to live among and to serve the East End poor. In fact, she had previously rejected the possibility of marriage for fear that it would distract her from this goal. Upon her engagement she immediately converted Barnett to her plan and, through the mediation of Octavia Hill, secured for him the offer of St. Jude's. It was an auspicious beginning for the woman who was always to be known in the parish as "the Vicaress".

The parish itself was less auspicious. Cheaply built between 1845 and 1848, the church served too small a district, an area later described by Barnett as "ten minutes long and three minutes wide." [18] Within these confines were crowded more than 6,000 people, many of them Jews, most of them slum-dwellers, half of them in want of the most basic necessity, food. Parochial activity itself was nearly non-existent, having been allowed to collapse during the long illness of the previous vicar. The parish schools were unused; the accounts did not even balance. With some justice the Bishop had called it the "worst parish" in his diocese. On their first Sunday the Barnetts ministered to a congregation of six or seven old women, all of whom expected doles as the price for their attendance.

Immediately upon their arrival the Barnetts abolished parochial doles and out-relief, substituting for them a local C.O.S. committee. Understandably, their decision was not a popular one; more than once their lives were threatened when the vicarage was besieged by importuning mobs. This unpopularity did not help them in their principal activity during that first year in Whitechapel: parish visiting. Both the Barnetts visited, usually separately, Barnett himself often dressed in mufti. Their reception sometimes depended on the amounts their hosts had previously extracted from the parish. "Crikey", one of Barnett's new parishioners exclaimed, "there's bust my old gel's chance of getting grub out of the Church." [19]

Two other activities claimed the Barnetts' immediate attention: repair of the church and formation of a staff. With money raised from the West End and perhaps their own funds as well, they thoroughly refurbished the church, removing its galleries, painting it with bright colors, and installing its first heating system. In this work they were aided by several unmarried women volunteers who had known the Barnetts earlier and who followed them from their previous parish in Marylebone. Soon they were joined by others. Barnett preached frequently in the West End, soliciting not only money but volunteers as well. Kate Potter, the sister of Beatrice Webb, served for eight years as a parish visitor and rent collector, bringing her sisters into the work with her. Pauline Townsend gave four days a week to Whitechapel for twenty-two years. And one remarkable woman, Marion Paterson, came to St. Jude's at the age of nineteen and devoted her entire life to service within the parish. Initially attracted by Barnett's preaching, she wrote to a girl-friend in 1876:

> He [Hugh Reginald Haweis, Vicar of St. James, Marylebone] brought in a clergyman from the East End who talked to us about all the poor sinners in the wretched courts and alleys of his parish, for he says they are more sinners than sufferers and want our friendship more than our money. I want to go and be their friend: I know they are drunkards and a worse class of people than I have ever seen, but I would try so hard to help them if only Papa

and Mamma will let me. Mr. Barnett does not want us to
be district visitors or preach to them or anything like
that, but be really a friend to them, and so perhaps lead
them to God without their knowing.

Henrietta Barnett confesses that the "Vicar's ladies" were always a family
joke, "for he had more women friends than any man I knew!" [20] An
occasional man did come to help, a curate joined the staff by 1877, and
soon the number of curates was expanded to three.

    The early staff was small, drawn largely from the C.O.S. cir-
cle around Octavia Hill. Yet they did a remarkable work, refurbishing the
church, re-opening the parish schools, beginning evening classes, host-
ing a variety of entertainments. At the end of their first year in Whitechapel, the Barnetts reported that:

> The congregation has risen to about thirty in mornings,
> and fifty to one hundred in the evenings; that a children's
> service has been started, and that a mixed choir is under
> training; that the schools have been opened for boys and
> girls together, of whom 142 are on the register; that adult
> classes have been started in French, German, Latin, arith-
> metic, composition, and drawing which have attracted fif-
> ty students; that a mothers' meeting has been begun, a
> nurse and a mission-woman engaged, a girls' night school
> carried on, a maternity society initiated, a penny bank
> opened, a lending library organized, a pension scheme in-
> augurated, a flower show held, concerts and entertain-
> ments given, oratorios rendered in Church, lady visitors
> set to work, and last but not least, a system of relief for
> the poor thought out and established.

Barnett never could have accomplished all this without his remarkable
ability to attract unpaid women volunteers. But neither could he have accomplished it without what his wife confesses was his "natural aptitude
for organising." [21]

    The early fruits of this organizational ability were concentrated
on the young: the re-opening of the parish schools and the founding of
youth clubs. Despite the failure of his brave plans for co-education, and
the consequent necessity of operating separate schools for boys and girls,
Barnett continued to innovate. As one early teacher reported, "We began

with soap, towels, and looking-glasses (unheard-of luxury) for the cloak-
room." [22] Classroom walls were decorated with colorful prints, flowers were distributed to the children throughout the summer months, and
the parents were asked to elect two of the schools' managers. The Barnetts always taught the classes in bible and began the school day with
staff prayers. Barnett himself frequently used the metaphor of "Holy
Communion" to describe what ought to take place in the classroom.

Alongside the schools, the Barnetts developed a series of clubs
and classes to keep older youngsters away from the temptations of the
streets. Afternoon classes, many in domestic arts, were aimed at girls too
old for school but too young for marriage. Six different clubs for girls
and young women were begun, and a gymnasium especially for girls was
opened in a local warehouse. Presumably, though there is no mention of
this in Barnett's biography, a parallel series of clubs were developed for
the boys. Finally, a "Play-class" for youngsters, both boys and girls, was
opened at the school every evening, since so many local families did not
provide any supervision to their children's activities.

For those families, Barnett worked to secure better housing.
Initially opposed to state aid, he convinced wealthy friends to purchase
local properties as they came on the market, refurbish them, and let them
out at reasonable rates. About 1875 Henrietta Barnett sold her inherited
jewelry in order to purchase such a block of tenements. Originally she
had hoped to secure the moral reformation of her tenants by establishing
a rigid set of qualifications for occupancy, but this lofty goal had to be
abandoned. "At last we decided that if we were to admit any applicants
from our parish, all we could demand was that the new tenants should not
earn their living by vice. [23] By 1879 one thousand people were living
in flats owned either by the Barnetts or by their West End friends. A vigorous supporter of the Artisans' Dwellings Act of 1875, Barnett also
helped found the East End Dwellings Company to secure the building of
new blocks in Whitechapel. The Whitechapel murders by "Jack the Rip-
per" in 1888, one of which occurred beside St. Jude's, served to focus national attention on the poor conditions of the district and gave rise to various proposals for state aid. Reluctantly Barnett came to the conclusion
that municipal housing was the only remedy for such a large scale problem, but he continued to believe that only individual action could right
the underlying social disease. "If the English people deeply felt for their
neighbours, they would have the will, and, having the will, they would
find the way to prevent the evils which are destroying and degrading hu-

man beings." [24]

Despite the proliferation of clubs and committees, the Barnetts' first commitment was to visiting, to serving as friends to the poor. To this end, they not only resided in Whitechapel, but they also lived on a severely restricted income, much less than the allowances from their respective families would have provided. Yet they still felt distant from the poor, and the poor did not come to church or turn to them in the numbers that the Barnetts had hoped. Henrietta Barnett argued that they should abandon the vicarage with its few servants and take rooms in one of Whitechapel's worst quarters. Her husband demurred, maintaining that with a large and secure income they could never experience the worst of poverty's insecurities. At any time they could abandon their arrangement, and never would they have to fear a pension-less old age. [25] But the argument apparently continued for some time as the Barnetts searched for new ways to meet their neighbors.

In their early years at St. Jude's the Barnetts had neither daily prayers nor a weekly communion. Rather, they concentrated their efforts on the traditional Sunday services, Morning and Evening Prayer, trying to enliven them with special music. But Barnett was no popular preacher. "On Mondays", his wife would say of his sermon, "it is simple, fit for a coster; on Saturday only a philosopher could understand it." [26] Participation in the developing list of parish organizations was never made contingent on church attendance, and thus few came, sometimes merely a handful, only rarely more than a hundred and fifty.

The Barnetts searched for new ways to make the church services attractive. Samuel Barnett attributed part of the failure to the liturgical rigidity of the Prayer Book, concluding that "No way seems to exist by which the spriritual side of people can be reached." [27] But it was his wife who pushed him in 1881 to develop a new Sunday evening service using music, contemporary readings, and extemporaneous prayer. Much of the church's nave was kept dark so the poor would not be embarrassed by their want of good clothes, and posters throughout the parish encouraged attendance for even a portion of the service. No sermon was given, the greater part being taken up with instrumental music, solos, and popular hymns from a specially-printed hymnal. "The Worship Hour", as the new service was termed, was clearly modeled on free church worship, both in its order and in its use of extemporaneous rather than set prayers. The Bishop, Walsham How, disagreed with the need for such a service, but was apparently won over by his respect for the Barnetts. And the

Worship Hour was a great success, attracting more worshippers than the regular services, sometimes as many as two hundred a week. To Barnett's great delight, the majority of these were among the poorer men. After attending anonymously one Sunday evening, Canon J. W. Horseley wrote to Barnett: "The men, as far as I could count, exceeded the women in the proportion of three to one, and were chiefly of the costermonger and low labouring class." [28]   Seven years after the service was begun, Barnett wrote: "Worship in which they themselves take part--prayers in the language of daily life and weighted with the thoughts of the day--music to express aspiration or sorrow not to be put into words--lessons from those scriptures which the Holy Spirit has never ceased to write for our learning, these are the means by which men of the nineteenth century may be helped to bind their failure with God's success, their weakness with His strength, and these are the means we have tried in our Worship Hour." [29]   By the end of his tenure at St. Jude's, Barnett had six regularly scheduled Sunday services. Yet the total attendance was never high, and Barnett never ceased despairing over the failure of his church to draw worshippers.

In an 1892 interview Barnett attributed the lack of church attendance to three causes: the wealth of the church, the coldness of its ritual, and its lack of democratic control. Episcopal palaces and princely stipends, he said, only convince the poor that the church is not their institution. They find it difficult to reconcile their own badly kept church and poorly paid parson with the affluence of parishes and clergy in the West End. Further, the services of the church are not only marked by "coldness and artificiality"; the ritual is in a language that the poor do not even understand. Finally, the poor do not feel the church is theirs because they have no control over the appointment of their ministers and little say in the parish activities.

Frequently Barnett called for reform of the church, arguing not for disestablishment but for a return to the "apostolic" precept that the people should choose their own teachers and govern their own parishes. "As the State is governed by the people for the people, the Church must be governed by the people for the people." [30]   Immediately upon coming to St. Jude's he tried to put this principle into effect by surrendering a large degree of authority to an elected Church Council of both men and women, a plan that Fremantle had adopted earlier at St. Mary's. The Council met once a month, planned the number and kind of services, decided upon decoration of the church, received complaints, and served as a committee of advice to the Vicar. There is no record of the Council's work, but in his appeal before the 1890 congregational election, Barnett wrote: "The committee as a rule are not masterful enough. They do not take the place of the people and say 'Here is our church, it shall be more useful to us.'" Barnett claimed that he had "given into the people's hands the management of the Church and the control of its services," but the people were not as ready as he hoped to assume those responsibilities. [31]

Culture Comes to Whitechapel

Despite its failure to attract worshippers, St. Jude's was an enormously busy parish, spawning a variety of activities that, in time, threatened to overwhelm the normal parochial structures. Some of these, such as the C.O.S. committee and the various housing associations, aimed directly to better the lives of the poor. Many of these, such as the parish schools, adult bible classes, mothers' meetings, boys' and girls' clubs, the medical club, and the temperance societies, were common to any highly organized East End parish of the time. But other activities were unique to St. Jude's. The Barnetts concentrated on bringing into the slums whatever was valued as beautiful or educational in the West End. An early colleague wrote:

> To those whose idea of the work of a parish was at all conventional, that at St. Jude's was a revelation. "Nothing short of the best" was the motto of whatever was attempted. . . . No one who was associated, even for a short time, and who entered into the spirit of its Vicar and his wife, could ever return to conventional ideas of Church life and Church work, or could fail to realize that all good social work is religious, and should be undertaken as part of God's service. [32]

Beginning with their very first year the Barnetts had organized a series of evening classes in English composition, foreign languages, and mathematics. Taught by volunteers from the West End, later by university students, these classes were ostensibly aimed at adults whose formal education had ended at an early age. The number of proffered sub-

jects expanded constantly until, by the end of the Barnetts' time in Whitechapel, it totaled one hundred thirty-four. Approximately half were una-
bashedly academic in nature, while the other half covered more practical
fields, such as dressmaking, bookkeeping, first aid, and contemporary
politics. Allied with the courses were a number of reading-parties that attempted to introduce working people to the best of English letters. Inevitably the Barnetts aimed too high. Though they sometimes had more
than 1,000 students registered for the various courses in a single year,
many of these were clerks and young teachers, hardly the Whitechapel
poor. Greater success was achieved at the end of the century, when ele-
mentary education classes were opened for men only. One hundred and
fifty working men signed up immediately. [33]

Almost as important as education, in the Barnetts' minds, was
the bringing of art and beauty into the East End. At first this desire focused on the church itself; a new organ was obtained, choirs were trained,
and the walls of St. Jude's were hung with religious paintings. Barnett
continued to hope that "with our new organ, with a building bright with
colour and pictures", larger congregations would be attracted. [34] Even
as late as 1891 the Vicar was still appealing in his parish magazine for
more paintings to decorate the church. From the beginning, however, additional concerts--outside the context of worship--were sponsored in the
church. Twice a month, generally alternating with the weeks during
which lectures were scheduled, a concert was presented, sometimes an or-
chestral work, but more frequently a vocal offering by artists whom the
Barnetts had persuaded to donate their talents. Oratorios were frequent,
and Handel's "Messiah" recurred with almost discouraging regularity.
"The Church music is gathering in people and perhaps souls . . . ," Barnett wrote in 1884. The creeds, he felt, had become divisive, symbolic
of the separation of the churches, but music was a parable, a unifying
force, "giving to all that feeling of common life" that had once been the
strength of the church. [35] Ironically, for he was always antagonistic to
ritualism, Barnett's decoration of the church and encouragement of choral
music soon raised suspicions that he was secretly an anglo-catholic.
More than once the police had to be called to prevent a "no-popery" riot
outside the chuch doors. But the protestants need not have worried; Barnett soon alienated the high churchmen by his practice of evening communions and by his introducing a mixed choir of men and women.

Shortly after coming to Whitechapel Barnett had written, "The
great want of this East End of London is beauty." [36] Decorating the

church could provide only a small oasis amidst the ugly streets and mean buildings. Thus the Barnetts resolved to move art out of the church. One of their earliest projects, that of providing mosaics for the blank walls of public buildings, never progressed far because of the expense, though several mosaics were later erected as memorials to the Vicar. Much more successful was their sponsorship of art shows. During the school's Easter vacation of 1881 the Barnetts opened an exhibition in the empty class-rooms of paintings borrowed from friends and museums. At last Barnett was pleased with the numbers he attracted to one of his projects; about 10,000 came during the nine days of the exhibition that first year. The art show became an annual event, attracting more than 25,000 people its second year and more than 55,000 by 1886, when three additional exhibi-tion rooms had been added to the parish schools for the purpose. Each year about 350 paintings were displayed, and each year the exhibition at-tracted greater notice in the press and further offers of artistic loans. Eventually the exhibitions led to the establishment of the Whitechapel Art Gallery, a museum that still sponsors pioneering exhibitions amidst a depressing block on Whitechapel High Street.

Barnett's own appreciation of art was not great. Congenitally color-blind, he always preferred the simple and allegorical paintings of G. F. Watts, but his wife was raised in a family to whom art was impor-tant, and it was she who took the lead in arranging for loans, in hanging the pictures, and in writing the catalogue. Noted artists of the day--Watts, Holman Hunt, Dante Rossetti, Burne-Jones, and Millais, among others-- were solicited; all responded with loans and many agreed to personal ap-pearances. Even Queen Victoria sent a painting from her personal collec-tion. Henrietta Barnett had high standards; she would not agree to exhibit paintings she considered to be of less than museum quality. She records that in 1893, when she was negotiating with Mrs. Alexander Young for the loan of some pictures, her hostess offered six or eight of the lesser canvases for the exhibition:

> "Thank you", I said, "I quite recognise your kindness, but I cannot accept them."
> "Not accept them--why not?" Mrs. Young asked with sur-prise.
> "Because they are not your best. If they were the best you possessed, it would be different; but with all these magnificant pictures which you could lend, I cannot take

your second-rate. The best must be lent for the service of
the poor. [37]

Mrs. Young did loan the best of her collection, including an Israels, a
Millet, a Corot, and a Jacques, necessitating a fifty thousand pound insu-
rance policy on just her portion of the exhibition.

The Barnetts' desire to introduce their neighbors to a better,
brighter world included entertainment. "My husband counted it a religious duty to give parties", wrote his widow. [38] And Barnett was never
one to shirk what he saw as duty. He believed that if only the poor and
the wealthy could really meet, they would learn a respect for one another
and discern a common interest that could eventually reform the inequities
of British society. "Those who break bread together with the poor," Barnett wrote, "still find that One is present who turns the meal into a Holy
Communion." [39] But Barnett was not without his many critics; his
early parochial reports are filled with explanations for the expense of his
entertainments. In his first such report, that for 1874, he wrote: "I would
justify it on two grounds: first, that such an expenditure naturally be-
longs to our whole system of dealing with the poor, and secondly, that
the religion of amusement has greatly been lost sight of." [40] Congregational parties, to which all parishioners were invited, were held monthly in the school's classrooms, since the vicarage was not large enough to
accommodate all who came. Here there were refreshments and music and
sometimes dancing as well. Barnett occasionally dressed in costume,
once playing Livingstone to his curate's Stanley.

To the congregational parties were added numerous gatherings
at the vicarage, engraved invitations being sent to parishioners and West
Enders alike. The "R.S.V.P." was often a cause of some wonder in
Whitechapel. "'Reserved seats, very pleased' was one of the suggested in-
terpretations, but it was soon explained, and was yet another tiny effort
to ignore class differences." [41] As some of the Barnetts' wealthy supporters met the poor, they responded with invitations to their own
homes. At first these efforts met with difficulties: some of the Whitechapel people would arrive drunk, while many would scramble for the
food or steal the fruit. But the Barnetts persisted, arguing that poor guests
must be treated exactly as the wealthy, that entertaining the poor was a
duty enjoined by the gospel. In 1886 Barnett wrote: "The habit of entertaining the poor is, I believe, growing. . . . They [the rich] are realising
that if they would follow their Master they must treat the poor as their

friends and entertain them with their best." During their years at St. Jude's, the Barnetts hosted more than 400 parties of general invitation, in addition to many smaller gatherings at the vicarage. [42]

The congregational parties were the origin of the first St.Jude's excursions. Each summer an all-day trip was planned for the party-goers, often to one of the schools or universities. In this way Benjamin Jowett, the Master of Balliol, entertained Whitechapel people, as did other heads of houses at both Oxford and Cambridge. The Barnetts were frequent travellers, believing with Victorian zeal that touring had a necessarily educational value. In 1888, therefore, they founded a Traveller's Club to facilitate low-cost visits abroad for its members. A lack of funds prevented any but the financially most favored working people from participating, however. More popular were the frequent trips to see theatrical productions in the West End. During the summer months, almost every St. Jude's organization scheduled frequent outings.

The most successful excursions were the two-week country holidays organized for the children. During the summer of 1877 the Barnetts arranged for nine of the poorest youngsters in their parish to lodge for a fortnight with rural families. Barnett wrote later that, "This plan of holiday-giving was begun not only for the sake of health and pleasure. There is truth in the old evangelical teaching that the chief object is salvation of souls, but salvation must be understood to mean the full development of human nature." [43] A letter to the **Guardian** elicited a list of country families willing to take children, money was raised, and by 1880 more than four hundred youngsters were sent on holiday. The scheme gave rise to the Children's Country Holiday Fund, a society chaired by Barnett until shortly before his death. By the time of the First World War a million children had been provided holidays, and the Fund had given rise to numerous parallel "fresh air funds" both on the Continent and in America.

Last Years at St. Jude's

Samuel Barnett is hardly remembered, if remembered at all, for his work as a parish clergyman. Rather, he is recalled as a social reformer, as a rather vague Christian who was animated by a zeal to serve the poor. And there is much in this view that is correct. Certainly Barnett himself recognized that his particular mission reached far beyond normal parochial concerns:

> It is almost impossible for a London clergyman to con-
> fine his work to his parish limits. He must take part in
> the management of societies from which the parishioners
> receive benefits, and he must set an example by doing his
> duty as a citizen. Among all the duties which London
> calls on its citizens to perform, none is above that of car-
> ing for the poor. [44]

Yet there is a sense in which this is only a partial view. Barnett considered himself a clergyman before all else. His wife writes that had he not
made the decision to accept the offer of St. Jude's, ". . . I doubt if his
mind would have turned in the direction it did. He would then have followed the inclination of his spirit, and taught the people religious truths.
It was because they were living under circumstances which precluded
them from receiving such truths, that he poured his whole life's force
into improving conditions." [45] Undoubtedly, Barnett's long-range contributions have been to social reform. But while he remained Vicar, St.
Jude's was one of the busiest of all East End parishes.

The Barnetts did not view their parish's activity as an unmixed
blessing. Frequently they protested the administrative demands made
upon them, feeling that they were being drawn ever further from their
work with individuals. So strongly did they fear this that, after a trip
around the world in 1890 and 1891, they resolved "to turn our backs on
beloved St. Jude's and on Toynbee with its brilliant society, glad eager
life, influential following, and troops of devoted friends, and go, just he
and I alone, farther east, and there, stript of the paraphernalia of a successful organisation, live side by side with the poor and the sad, and reach after their souls." [46] Barnett took their plan to the Bishop of London,
then Frederick Temple, requesting that they be assigned a remote district
of the East End, where they would take responsibility for raising money,
building a church, and caring for the people's souls. But Temple apparently did not take the offer seriously. Reading his correspondence
throughout the interview, he simply remarked that the Barnetts would
never be able to escape their following and promised to answer by letter.
The stipulated letter never arrived, a fact that disappointed Barnett and
may have hastened his resolve to leave St. Jude's. "We rarely spoke

about it; for Mr. Barnett was too pained and I was too indignant to make discussion on the subject fruitful for good. But it added to his humility that his Bishop had not thought his offer worthy of consideration, and my husband's humility was a flower that became unhealthy if too much watered." [47]

By this time St. Jude's had spawned more than fifty parish clubs and committees. The bulk of these involved children or young people, for Barnett, like other East End clergymen, was primarily concerned to rescue youngsters from a life of poverty, and the youth seemed more tractable and susceptible of organization. The Evening Home, the Girls' Club, and the Boys' Guild were probably the busiest of all the associations; they provided activities every night of the week for youngsters of all ages. By keeping them off the streets, and by training their minds and bodies, the Barnetts felt that they were preparing the children for a better life and thus for the Kingdom of God.

The impression given by the sixty issues of the parish magazine is one of exhausting hyperactivity. Organizations had spawned committees, and the committees had proliferated until every night of the week was marked by meetings at each possible location--the church, the schools, the vicarage, the associated Toynbee Hall, and various other rented quarters. Of course, the Barnetts were not active in all the societies and committees, but the administrative burden must have been considerable, especially for a couple who believed the cornerstone of their work to be association with individuals. Barnett admitted as much in the first issue of *St, Jude's* when he confessed that ". . . .we can no longer daily or weekly meet our friends. . . ." [48] For the Barnetts themselves, and probably for their parishioners as well, the parish magazine was a poor substitute. Yet Barnett would not draw back from his attempts to organize, for he believed that Anglican clergy had a different mission from that of either Roman Catholic or free church pastors: "they are ministers not to a sect, but to the people; and yet they have no means of knowing those to whom they are sent; they cannot study, they can hardly pray, because their time is taken up with efforts "to get hold of the people." [49]

Though attendance was never great, the Barnetts--together with their three curates and twenty-five Sunday School teachers--maintained an active Sunday Schedule. By 1890 there were six services on Sunday, including at least one communion, a men's service, a children's service, and the Worship Hour, besides Morning and Evening Prayer. In addition each of the Barnetts taught bible classes on Sunday afternoon. Four different sermons were delivered each Sunday, with an additional talk at a Wednesday evening service, Holy Days were apparently not celebrated, but the church was kept open daily from 11 a.m. to 5 p.m. for private prayer, daily services during Holy Week were begun in 1891, and a daily devotional service for parish workers was started in 1892. And Barnett never ceased pleading with his parishioners to come more frequently to communion: "The most sacred service that we have in Church and the most solemn act of our life as a Christian family at St. Jude's is the Sacrament of the Lord's Supper, or the Holy Communion." [50] But the people did not come in any large numbers to the communion; the only services at St. Jude's that could be termed popular were Evening Prayer and the Worship Hour. Barnett himself might be a sacramentalist, but he did not manage to communicate the same attitude to his neighbors.

Barnett was not only disappointed; he was also tired. In 1884 he had founded the first settlement house, an attempt to bring university graduates to live as neighbors and friends of the poor. And though Toynbee Hall was associated with St. Jude's, his duties as Warden of the one and Vicar of the other had proven too great a strain on his own health and that of his wife. His old friend Benjamin Jowett, who had long counselled resignation from the parish, finally secured for Barnett an offer of a canonry at Bristol, Barnett's birthplace. Henrietta Barnett later wrote, ". . . the noise, dirt and sadness of Whitechapel and the strain of the dual duties of Vicar of St. Jude's and Warden of Toynbee Hall were very trying, and we welcomed Lord Herschell's gift of a Stall at Bristol in 1893."[51] For the next thirteen years, however, the Barnetts continued to maintain their permanent residence in Whitechapel, and Barnett retained his wardenship of Toynbee Hall. Until 1898 he continued to serve St. Jude's as senior curate as well.

The Politics of Service

Throughout his twenty-three years in Whitechapel, Barnett was constantly involved in political controversy. His wife later reported that her husband, like most young men, enjoyed fighting and had a mind that was ". . . so constituted that, as soon as anything had become established, he wanted to reform it." [52] The burden of this reforming zeal was directed to local causes, for though Barnett chafed constantly at national politics, he never endorsed particular candidates in the general elections. Within a year of coming to St. Jude's he became a Guardian of the Poor Law and a Manager of the local Board (state) School, both positions bringing him into contact with local politics. And he did campaign extensively to get candidates with whom he sympathized elected to the Board, the one local political office he regarded as the most critical.

The other area of local political controversy involving the Barnetts were the strikes that began in the mid-eighteen-eighties. Without endorsing all the strikers' demands, Barnett invariably took their side. The great dock strike of 1889 became the watershed of labor relations in the East End. When it began the Barnetts were on a summer holiday in Switzerland, but they hurried home upon receiving the news in early August. Abandoning their stand against out-relief, they provided food and pensions to the striking dock workers. At the same time, Barnett wrote to his brother, "My feelings are with the men, but how to give those feelings expression is more than I know." [53]

On the whole, the Church of England came off rather badly as the strike continued through September. The dockers, four-fifths of whom were Irish, appealed to the Anglican Bishop of London and the Roman Catholic Bishop of Westminister for support. After a brief attempt at mediation, Bishop Temple left for a holiday in Wales; but Cardinal Manning stayed with the negotiations and eventually proved instrumental in securing a settlement. Meanwhile the Barnetts were entertaining the Central Strike Committee in their home and continuing their public support of the strikers. After the settlement, Ben Tillett, the Congregationalist strike leader, had words of praise for the Roman Catholics but little good to say of the Established Church, except for Barnett. [54]

Barnett was encouraged by the strike, for in his view it taught the workers discipline and self-confidence. While the strike was still in progress, the parish magazine carried articles on the lessons of the labor uprising: "Two things, though, the strike has already done for the men of the East End--and they are of more value than many sixpences: it has increased their manliness, it has taught them self-reliance." [55] Six months later, however, Barnett retreated into his typical worried pose. Though the dockers had won, he wrote:

> Somehow without any evidence I have a sense of anxiety
> about the Docks. I don't like either the feeling of directors

> or dockers. The first don't believe in the Union, the last
> don't know what Union demands. . . . In the end labour
> must win, but like Napoleon in Russia it may be in a
> field on which it will starve. [56]

From the time of the dock strike, Barnett became closely identified with the unions' cause, frequently addressing their gatherings and constantly loaning both Toynbee Hall and the St. Jude's schools for their meetings. But he continued to insist that the strikers had a responsibility to better their lives. During the "coal war" of 1893 he wrote: "If only the men had not spent so much of their wages in drink, and so much of their leisure in brutal sport!" [57]

On the national level, Barnett had refused to lend his public support to particular candidates. [58] Originally a Liberal, he moved--partly through the influence of the strikers--to the quiet support of the fledgling Labour Party. By 1902, when he addressed a Labour gathering in Bristol, he was willing to be publicly identified with the new party: "My hope, as an Englishman and a patriot, lies with the labour party." [59] Characteristically he went on to warn the working men against greed, arguing that they must act on the principle of cooperation rather than exploitation. In another place he suggested that the English working class was narrow-minded and xenophobic, and that a Labour government might destroy Britain's foreign alliances. [60]

Barnett's most unequivocal stands on national issues all involved questions of war and peace. Though he did not use the term of himself, Barnett was a pacifist. Shortly after coming to Whitechapel, he sponsored a public meeting to protest the jingoistic agitation for war against Russia, an unpopular meeting that was broken up by his detractors. Later, he intensely disliked the American President Theodore Roosevelt, writing that, "It [war] is opposed equally to reason, to experience, and to the Christian spirit." [61] After his 1891 trip around the world he became just as acerbic on the subject of the British Empire. There could be no trust between the colonial governors and the governed native people, he said. "Suspicion, self-distrust, and deceitfulness are common in India and they belong to the spirit of the conquered, as surely as arrogance, presumption, and brutality belong to the spirit of the conquerer." [62] But it was the Boer War that incited his strongest revulsion. The spectacle of "Africans shot down by English guns" was one he thought any Christian must condemn. [63] Even within the narrow con-

fines of Toynbee Hall, however, few followed his lead; sixteen of the
twenty residents supported the war and opposed Barnett. "On some evenings we deemed it better not to dine in [Toynbee] Hall . . ." his wife recalled of that period." [64]

The most interesting question concerning Barnett's politics is
whether or not he was a socialist. Owen Chadwick accepts his 1883 es-
pousal of "practicable socialism" as proof that Barnett had finally moved
into the camp of the "Christian Socialists" where he, like the other followers of Maurice, had so many natural ties. [65] There were numerous
pressures on Barnett to declare himself a socialist; since much of his
thought tended in that direction, his detractors accused him of dishonesty
for not earlier avowing the title. He was surrounded by people who had
already declared themselves; Charles Marson, a noted Christian Socialist
of the next generation, served his first curacy under Barnett. But Barnett
never called himself a socialist without inserting "practicable" or another
qualifying phrase before the critical appellation. And he never joined the
Christian Social Union or any other, even vaguely, socialist body.

Barnett's socialism, like many of his social views, was of a
distinctly idiosyncratic sort. In his 1883 article he rejected the current socialistic schemes, particularly those derived from continental sources, as
"impracticable." What was needed, he wrote later, was not a neat political
solution, but a way of helping the poor become self-reliant so that they
might be "good governors as well as good workmen and servants." By itself, socialism would do little to correct the underlying problems in the
East End. Only through personal influence would the poor be raised up
until they were no longer spiritually and culturally, as well as financially, impoverished. "I do not say", Barnett wrote, "Be socialist or individu-
alist, . . . I simply repeat the command 'Love God'. . . .A religion of the
nineteenth century would make a philanthropy of the nineteenth century."
[66] Ultimately, Barnett was a philanthropist rather than a socialist. He
would have been happier with the former title. But he lived in a time
when not to be a socialist would have been to disavow not only many of
his supporters, but also the progressive spirit of the age that so encouraged him. Thus Barnett declared himself. He became perhaps the most
hesitating, reluctant, and apolitical socialist of his time. Following his
lead, a co-worker wrote in the parish magazine: "London is still a long
way from an ideal 'Socialism', but we have some Practical Socialists in
East London who believe in 'Socializing'--in other words, sharing--with
their neighbours the pleasure which the Whitechapel Fine Art exhibition

gives them." [67] That is precisely what Barnett understood his socialism to be: a practical means of sharing the good things of this world
with the poor who knew so little that was good. To espouse an economic
solution to poverty would have been, in Barnett's view, to shirk responsibility. Poverty was much more than a financial condition; its elimina-
tion would demand far more than economic solutions.

The Barnetts: An Assessment

It is not easy to recall the Barnetts today without smiling. In
retrospect their particular vision seems almost as implausible as Beatrice
Webb's first recollections of the improbable vicar. A Christian faith
broad enough to encompass the religious intimations of the agnostic, a
parish system built around party-giving, a conviction that the Kingdom
of God would arrive in the twentieth century, an incredible optimism
about human nature, a corresponding blindness to man's willful destruc-
tiveness, all these combine to make the Barnetts seem a rather bizarre
eruption into the normal parish life of their day. Yet there is a certain
glory in absurdity, and if the Barnetts were absurdly quixotic, at least
they were quixotic with a style unmatched in their generation. No one
believed more firmly in the possibility of ordinary men and women to effect their own salvation. No one worked any harder, or with any less pre-
possessing mortals, to prove that conviction. Ultimately the Barnetts
failed in the task they had set for themselves. But the advantage of hind-
sight, the knowledge of what the twentieth century actually produced,
should not blind the modern observer to the nobility of their attempt, nor
to their very real, if unintended, accomplishments

Samuel Barnett came to Whitechapel with a vitiated Maurician
theology, vitiated because it lacked Maurice's sense of Christ's atonement
and because it failed to account for the depth of human sinfulness. But
what his theology lacked Barnett made up for by the intensity of his faith
in the saving power of individual effort and by his conviction that the
Kingdom of God was breaking in upon the kingdom of man. His commission was to teach, for it was only by education that men and women
could overcome their selfishness and thereby participate in the new age.
The life of Jesus, the lives of the heroes in every era, the art and music of
the West End, the studies of the universities, all these the Barnetts attempted to teach their neighbors. The high walls and the narrow streets

of Whitechapel signified far more than merely economic deprivation. For the Barnetts they symbolized as well the even greater spiritual poverty of culture and intellect. It was this spiritual poverty, more than any other, that entrapped the East End. If the poor were to be truly liberated, they would require not doles but education, not aid but respect, not the hand-me-downs of West End affluence but the best of West End culture. "The best must be lent for the service of the poor." It was a glorious, if unintendedly patronizing, vision.

The Barnetts went to extremes to avoid patronizing their neighbors. More seriously than any other churchmen of their time, they considered abandoning the isolation of the vicarage in order to share the general poverty of the East End. As earnestly as any others, they tried to befriend the poor without reserving to themselves the aloofness of condescension. From the "R.S.V.P." on their engraved invitations to the principles of the C.O.S., they tried to treat their neighbors as equals. And yet they failed. The Barnetts, with every intention to the contrary, could not help but patronize the poor, for they could not accept the poor as they were. To the Vicar and his wife, there was no genuine Cockney culture worthy of respect, nothing but the courage and self-sacrifice of particular individuals in the East End. At a time when clergymen in the foreign mission fields were learning to be anthropologists, the Barnetts had no such self-doubts. Their vision was clear. As missionaries from the upper middle class, their duty was to socialize the Whitechapel natives to West End culture. Their goal was, as Samuel Barnett expressed it in his hope for the parish schools, "to teach manners and courteous behaviour, so that . . . the children may grow up as ladies and gentlemen." [68]

To this end the Barnetts developed one of the most extensive parochial systems known in the East End. With the help of the Toynbee Hall residents, their staff was larger, their organizations more numerous, and their concerns more far-reaching than those of all but two or three other East End parishes of their time. And yet, in large measure, the people did not come to church. Unlike his contemporary slum vicars, Barnett refused, as a matter of principle, to use membership in the parish organizations to bribe his parishioners into church-going. And so they did not come. Always inclined to melancholy, Barnett judged himself a failure in this important part of his work. He was a failure, for there is little evidence that he made the church--as the church, and not merely as a school or social agency--a vital part of his neighbors' lives. The most he could say in 1898, when he left the parish altogether, was that clergymen in the East End were now respected rather than reviled: "It is no longer a popular thing to abuse the parson . . . ." [69] After he left St. Jude's even his small congregation dwindled away. The Bishop of London judged the parish redundant in 1923, and the church itself was demolished.

But even if Barnett failed in the most narrow definition of his work as a clergyman, he was an outstanding success in every broader description of that role. In many ways Barnett was a typical broad churchman. He was not an idiosyncratic exception, for much of the early organization at St. Jude's was modelled directly upon Fremantle's work in Marylebone: the C.O.S. committee, the democratically elected parish council, a program to train girls for service. What was unique to Barnett was his easy equation of religion with education and cultural pursuits, but this was a tendency, at least, shared by all those of the school that looked to Maurice for inspiration. As a broad churchman Barnett had few real colleagues in the East End, for no contemporary of his theological persuasion tried to make his parish the center of reform. St. Jude's under Barnett will always stand as the example of what a missionary broad churchman might accomplish in the slums.

And Barnett accomplished a good deal. Without intending to separate social service from religious concerns, he laid the foundations for much of modern social work. Without being personally radical, he helped make political socialism a respectable stance for the Christian. And perhaps most importantly, he induced a cadre of women co-workers, some of whom were not even Christians, to join him in Whitechapel. In an era when women were subordinated, his conviction of their equality and his expectations from them helped change their view of themselves and society's estimation of their place. His own ministry cannot be separated from that of his wife. Samuel and Henrietta Barnett together demonstrate the strengths and the weaknesses of the broad church party. Their vague, immanentalist Christian faith infected few of their Whitechapel neighbors. But their insistence that the salvation of souls could not be separated from the salvation of minds and bodies affected a legion of young ordinands. And at the last day, the Barnetts would insist that their work be judged by their efforts for individuals. No one in the East End did more to make their people's lives "happier and brighter" than they.

IV

THE EVANGELICALS

There were evangelicals in the East End, though they were not nearly as numerous nor as well publicized as the anglo-catholics. William Quekett, the evangelical vicar of Christ Church, Watney Street, became known in the eighteen-forties for founding schools and for building St. Mary's, Cable Street. Ironically, St. Mary's is today one of the most anglo-catholic of all East End parishes. By the end of the century, Christ Church, Spitalfields, had an evangelical reputation, though one not associated with the name of any particular rector. But these were exceptions. It is possible that there were additional evangelical vicars who--partly because they were less controversial than the anglo-catholics--left little record of their work. But just as likely an explanation for their paucity is that the evangelical clergymen found it difficult to distinguish themselves from the low churchmen who held most East End benefices until the century's end. G. R. Balleine writes of the church in Whitechapel in 1837:

> The dingy old church had no influence whatever on the 36,000 people who were crowded round it. For thirty years the Low Church Rector, who had just died, had unlocked the church door every Sunday morning, read the service and a sermon to the clerk and the charity children, and then gone home to his mid-day dinner with the comfortable feeling that the week's work was satisfactorily accomplished. He had no curate, did no visiting, and apparently never tried to get in touch with his parishioners. [1]

Low churchmanship was the rule, as were non-resident clergy. It was not until later in the century that the evangelicals began to distinguish themselves from that East End norm.

There never were a sufficient number of evangelical clergy to

form a party in the East End. But two names do stand out: William
Weldon Champneys, Rector of St. Mary Matfelon, Whitechapel. from
1837 to 1860, and John Edwin Watts-Ditchfield, Vicar of St. James-the-
Less, Bethnal Green, from 1897 to 1914. Both chose the designation
"evangelical" rather than "low church", both developed extensive parochial organizations, and both were enormously successful in attracting worshippers.

William Weldon Champneys

Champneys is often cited as the leading evangelical of mid-
nineteenth century London, but remarkably little is known about his
ministry. After an outstanding six-year curacy at St. Ebbe's in Oxford,
where he established the first national schools in that city, earned a reputation for visiting the sick during the cholera epidemic of 1832, and held
a fellowship at Brasenose College, he was appointed to the College living of St. Mary Matfelon at the age of thirty, The son and grandson of
distinguished London clergymen, he was to be made a Canon of St.
Paul's in 1851, Vicar of St. Pancras in 1860, and Dean of Lichfield in
1868. He was also to father Sir Francis Champneys, the physician, and
Basil Champneys, the architect.

The Whitechapel parish to which Champneys came in 1837
was the second oldest in East London, the original church having been
constructed in the mid-thirteenth century as a chapel-of-ease to St. Dunstan's, Stepney. Yet its venerability belied its present health. Since at
least the late eighteenth century the parish had been served by a lone non-
resident clergyman who had contented himself with officiating at a single
Sunday service. Indeed, a careful reading of the meagre parish records suggests the last indications of parochial health occurred not long after the
Revolution of 1688. In a manuscript book of the "Rector's privilidges
and duties", begun in 1648 and now kept in the Greater London Record
Office, John Davie, Rector from 1750 to 1756, recorded:

> But besides this, as I am informed, a certain number of
> Persons calling themselves a Religious Society applied to
> Dr. Welton then Rector [1697-1714] for leave to have a
> Weekly sacrament and also prayers at 3 o'clock in the
> evening every Saturday; which was complied with they

being at the expense of Bread and Wine, and allowing to
the Curate 2.6 out of the Offering Money, and 2.2 to the
Clerk and Sexton *etc* for their attendance on such days.
This weekly Sacrament is still continued notwithstanding the Society is long ago ceased and the Offering
money not sufficient to defray the charges of it, so that
the Curate is yearly out of Pocket in order to support it,
besides his additional Labor of Attendance.

Since Dr. Welton was a high churchman who was later to become a non-
juring bishop in America, the style of piety he fostered is hardly surprising. But the piety was clearly embarassing to Welton's successors. Roger Mather, Rector from 1757 to 1768, recorded in the same manuscript
book:

Note, upon the Repair of the Church in 1764 I took the
opportunity of bringing back the Office of Communion
to the ancient Usage of the Parish, viz, once a month,
having found the Weekly Sacrament liable to many objections.

Between Mather and Champneys there were five incumbents, all non-
resident, none leaving any memory of vigorous parochial activity.

Champneys approached Whitechapel with the same energy that
had characterized his ministry at St. Ebbe's. Within a few years of his arrival he had founded separate schools for infants, for boys, and for girls.
Finding that many children were not attending these for want of the required clothing, he then established the first ragged school in London.
Champneys co-operated in forming two refuges, or homes, within the
parish: one for orphaned or abandoned boys who worked as shoe-blacks,
and one for fallen women. He instituted a savings society, assisted in the
building of the Whitechapel Foundation Commercial School, and promoted a local chapter of the Church of England Young Men's Society.
Like so many of the later East End clergy, the focus of his activity was
young people. Of the 33,000 people in Whitechapel, the majority were
poor, subject to the vagaries of casual labor. The most Champneys
could hope for was to redeem a proportion of his young parishioners
from their culture of poverty.

The British Museum lists more than fifty books published
over Champneys' name, large numbers of which are directed to children.

All are short; many are those he edited or to which he merely contributed a preface; none elucidates his work in Whitechapel. Champneys never wrote about his experience in the East End. The clearest statement he did make came twenty years after he became Rector of St. Mary's, in the annual report of one of the leading evangelical associations:

> We want a place of worship which the people shall feel to be *their own;* we want the sick to be visited; we want the poor to be specially cared for, and to be able to say amidst all their cares, "Well, we have something in England, we have our own Church and our own parson." [2]

With aid from another evangelical association, the Church Pastoral Aid Society, Champneys set about this goal with remarkable success. Two curates visited from door to door. A Sunday School was founded. Three services--morning, afternoon, and evening--were held on Sunday, together with one mid-week service. And the parishioners responded to this increased activity. In the Religious Census of 1851, St. Mary's recorded 1547 people present for the morning service, 827 in the afternoon, and another 1643 in the evening. Most of his congregation, Champneys maintained, came from the genuinely poor classes of Whitechapel. With considerable justice Leonard Elliott Binns calls Champneys "the pioneer of the modern type of town parson" and Charles Bullock termed him "the model working clergyman." [3]

Yet Champneys differed in one significant respect from the many active clergy who were to follow him into the East End: he did not live within his parish. Rather, he left the day-to-day work of the church in his curates' hands, concentrating his own efforts on administration, on his duties as rural dean of Stepney, and on his participation in the several national evangelical associations. Indeed, the only surviving service book from the time of his tenure at St. Mary's indicates that Champneys preached there only once during the last thirteen years of his rectorate. On 2 March 1849 Champneys preached at the morning service on Acts 7:59-60, a text that concludes with the words, "And when he had said this, he fell asleep." [4] Champneys hardly fell asleep at St. Mary's. In many ways he was the pioneer, whether those who followed him acknowledged his leadership or not, of a new style of slum ministry. Yet he differed from those who came later in one respect that they considered vital to such a ministry. By not living within his parish and leading its work personally, he was a precursor rather than the founder of the late nineteenth century style of slum ministry.

John Edwin Watts-Ditchfield: Early Life

When Watts-Ditchfield came to the East End in 1897, he--like Champneys sixty years before--was a young evangelical clergyman who had just completed a remarkable curacy. But there the similarity ended. For almost alone among the prominent slum clergy of his own and the preceding generation, Watts-Ditchfield came from a family that was at best marginally middle-class. His biographer, who was also his son-in-law and former curate, says that Watts-Ditchfield was born in 1861 at Patricroft, near Manchester, to a Wesleyan family noted for its industry and piety. The elder Ditchfield had gone to work at the age of eight in a local cotton mill. [5] Despite the rigors of twelve-and-a-half hour days, the father had somehow completed his education, earned a schoolmaster's certificate, and gained a position as headmaster of the Patricroft Higher Grade School. There seemed little thought of sending John Edwin to university; rather, he was directed from an early age toward teaching and, if possible, the Wesleyan ministry. The first goal was accomplished, yet when Watts-Ditchfield presented himself for ordination in 1887 and again in 1888, both the Wesleyan Methodist Conference and the Wesleyan Mission House refused his application. Apparently in despair of securing ordination from Wesleyan hands, he was confirmed in the Church of England at Manchester Cathedral in late 1888, and--so his biographer says-- shortly thereafter accepted an invitation to come to London and become secretary to the Vicar of St. Stephen's, North Bow. [6]

Unfortunately, the biography was edited by Watts-Ditchfield's widow, a woman of some social pretension, who heavily censored the chapters dealing with her late husband's early life. Watts-Ditchfield's daughter and grandson insist that his origins were considerably more humble than Gowing has indicated, that he attended Manchester University but failed to take a degree, that he was rejected for the Wesleyan ministry because of delicate health, and that after securing Anglican confirmation he journeyed to London, impecunious and unemployed. His daughter says that later in life Watts-Ditchfield often marvelled at the contrast between his current position as Bishop and the despair of his early days in London. [7] Despite his lack of prospects, however, he did locate a position as secretary, from whence he proceeded to ordination in 1891 and to St. Peter's, Upper Holloway, where he was to serve his title under a well-known vicar, J. F. Osborne.

Watts-Ditchfield proved a remarkable curate. The two keys to his effectiveness, parish visiting and a special service for the men, were developed from the beginning of his ministry. "Get to know the men" was probably his most frequently repeated injunction, and this he did at St. Peter's. The parish magazine reported after his death more than thirty years later, "The curate certainly had strange ideas: he actually thought it his duty to know about everything that was being done in the parish . . . ." [8] Though an almost militant teetotaler, he haunted the Upper Holloway public houses during the day, confining most of his parish calling to the evening, when the men would be at home. Nine months after coming to the parish, Watts-Ditchfield began his Sunday afternoon services for men only as a response to "the great need for a service, at once bright, hearty, and simple, to which men of all classes could be invited, and at which they could be made to feel at home." One hundred and twenty men came to the first service, their numbers shortly rising to about 800 every week. [9] In his second annual report on the men's service, Watts-Ditchfield amplified its purpose:

> The aim and object of this service is to lead men through Christ to a higher, purer, and nobler life in God, and to prove that Christianity is not a failure, but the one thing that can make a true man--a gentlenan, indeed, in the highest sense--one who is all that he ought to be in himself, and does all that he ought to do for his brother men. To accomplish this, the character of the service is distinctly a religious one, while at the same time it is one in which all can join, and which all can thoroughly enjoy. [10]

Watts-Ditchfield's success gained him a certain degree of publicity. In 1895 he had refused an offer of a living in Wolverhampton partly because ". . . having made a somewhat special study of London problems and their peculiar difficulties, I ought not to throw away the experience thus gained." [11] Thus it was no surprise when, in 1897, the Bishop of London offered him the parish of St. James-the-Less, Bethnal Green. Watts-Ditchfield felt he had no choice but to accept.

St. James-the-Less: Parochial Organization

St. James-the-Less was a mid-nineteenth century parish created
in the northeastern corner of Bethnal Green, a crowded district of about
11,000 working people, many of whom were dockers, piece-workers, or
casual laborers. Located near Victoria Park, they could look across to the
Hackney Marshes and the new, middle-class suburbs developing little
more than a mile away. The church was in almost as bad a condition as
the local housing. Cold, badly lighted, and rather dilapidated, it had only
a small congregation, many of whom were drawn from the attached girls'
school. At Watts-Ditchfield's induction service, the Archdeacon said:

> . . . he is a man of so much zealous energy, that if you
> do not help him, he will soon wear himself out. In this
> parish there ought to be five curates; but this is impossi-
> ble. We cannot aim at such a high ideal. If your Vicar
> should have two curates it is as much as we can expect,
> but he should find among you many helpers. [12]

The Archdeacon was no prophet. Within a very few years, the Vicar was
to have between five and eight curates, together with a large staff of lay
assistants.

Watts-Ditchfield's first act was to build. During his curacy at
St. Peter's he had proved an enormously successful money-raiser. These
talents he now turned to the benefit of his new parish. Within three and
a half years he had raised 29,300 pounds, all from outside Bethnal Green,
most from individuals in the West End. With this he refurbished the
Church, constructed a large parish hall with a gymnasium and small
class-rooms, and created a parish garden, complete with tennis courts, a
band-stand, and a cycling path. The girls' school was converted into a
medical mission, while three neighboring houses were bought and made
over into the "Working Men's Hotel." Yet this did not satisfy Watts-
Ditchfield, for he believed--so his biographer says--that even in so small
a parish, distance from the church was preventing the attendance of some
who might otherwise come to services. A mission was therefore opened
in the poorest part of the parish, on Cranbrook Road. It was moved in
1902 to a disused chapel on Sidney Street. Finally, seven years after he

came to the parish, Watts-Ditchfield inaugurated Ridley House, a settlement house modeled on Toynbee Hall that provided a place for university
men, clergymen, and others who wished to come and view life in the
East End at first hand. Obviously, such an active parochial organization
required a large staff. The only surviving copy of the *St. James-the-Less
Monthly Magazine*, that for January 1912, list a full-time staff of five
curates and fifteen lay people, together with many part-time volunteers.
[13]

From the beginning of his ministry at St. James-the-Less,
Watts-Ditchfield began a vigorous program of parish visiting. Even a few
years ago, older parishioners could still recall seeing him constantly in
the streets. [14] As the staff grew, the parish was subdivided into districts, for each of which a curate and a lady helper were made responsible.
A visiting book for every district contained the name of each family and
their children, together with notes about their attitude toward religion. At
the weekly staff meetings, each assistant was required to report to the Vicar the visits he or she had made.

Within a month of taking over the parish, Watts-Ditchfield introduced the Sunday afternoon Men's Service that he had developed at St.
Peter's. He prepared for this with some agressive advertising concentrated
on the local publicans. An hour and a half before the service, the Vicar
assembled a brass band and toured a portion of the parish, handing out
printed invitations, stopping at every important street corner and before
each of the public houses for the Vicar to give a short address. In this
way, the band covered the whole parish every month. Within a short
time, the service was attracting seven hundred men each week. [15] The
Men's Service itself followed a very simple format. Neither the Book of
Common Prayer nor an Anglican hymnal was used. Rather, a small or-
chestra supported the singing of hymns from Sankey's book. Watts-
Ditchfield preached extemporaneously for about thirty minutes, and the
service concluded with simple prayers and the blessing.

Gowing has written, "The Men's Service was looked upon as
the normal means by which men were led to Christ." [16] Certainly it
spawned a large number of parish organizations, the most important of
which was the Men's Club. This was organized by a committee elected
from the Men's Service and was restricted to the members of the Sunday
afternoon congregation. It aimed to provide activities for men every
evening of the week as an alternative to the public house. Billiards, bag-
atelle, draughts. chess, and some forms of card games were held each

night in the parish hall, with the twin restrictions that there be no alcohol and no gambling on the premises. The Men's Club also organized several other societies all aimed at promoting thrift: a "Sick, Burial. and Annual Division Society", a Coal Club, a Loan Society, a savings club, and a Christmas Club. At the end of the Vicar's first year in Bethnal Green, these various societies had enrolled over 800 members. [17]

Although the Men's Service attracted Watts-Ditchfield's greatest attention, it was by no means the only service at St. James-the-Less. The 1912 parish magazine lists a morning and an evening service on Sunday, together with prayer meetings on Wednesday and Saturday nights. In addition, the Communion was celebrated at least once every Sunday morning, five times on the first Sunday of the month, twice on the third Sunday, once every Wednesday, and twice each Holy Day. It was a schedule with which even an anglo-catholic might not be too embarrassed.

At St. Peter's, the Men's Service had given rise to a parallel service for women only on Tuesday afternoons. This, too, was continued in Bethnal Green, and after some experimentation found its place in the parish schedule on Monday evenings. But Watts-Ditchiield's interest was not there; rarely does he mention the Women's Service, Rather, he frequently refers to his occasional forays in open-air preaching. Occasionally on Sunday mornings he would gather a small band and venture into the costermonger district of his parish on Green Street. Here, after a lively Sankey hymn, he would preach a short, extemporaneous address to a surprised and unintended congregation. In the same way, on summer Sunday evenings, he would take a portion of his regular congregation to the gates of the adjoining Victoria Park, where they would sing and he would preach to those returning from an afternoon's outing.

Perhaps Watts-Ditchfield's favorite activities, certainly those best remembered by his daughter, were two annual events for children: the Robin Dinners and the Sunday School Outing. The first was a Christmas dinner for 1000 of the poorest youngsters in the parish, held in two sittings at the parish hall. Here, while the children feasted on steak-and-kidney pie, the Vicar would address them in a simple sermon. The second was, according to Watts-Ditchfield's daughter, "the great day of the whole Year." More than thirty large wagons would transport the Sunday School children to Epping Forest for a day of picnicking and games. The entire parish would turn out to greet the returning children, illuminating their evening way home with "fairy lights" (candles placed within bottles) all along St. James' Road. The Sunday School, like the Men's Service, spawned its coterie of associated organizations, several of which were temperance societies. The Children's Guild held games on Monday nights, while the Lad's Club and the Girl's Club met throughout the week. For older children there were bible Classes, rigidly segregated by sex, with their attendant clubs. The Young Men's Guild, open to those boys who attended the bible Class at the Sidney Street Mission, sponsored at least ten different athletic teams. The Young Women's Guild concentrated on classes in home-making, with additional instruction offered in singing and elocution. In addition, there were parish troops of the Church Lads' Brigade. the Boy Scouts, and the Girl Guides. The organizations proliferated until, by the time of the 1912 parish magazine, more than forty such groups are listed.

The effects of all this vigorous parish activity are difficult to measure. The only surviving quantified data are the figures for Sunday School attendance, for confirmations, and for Easter Day communicants. In 1897, before Watts-Ditchfield had come to the parish, there was no Sunday School, and Easter Day communions numbered only twenty-six. By 1914. when Watts-Ditchfield left the parish to become Bishop of Chelmsford, the Sunday Schools had an average attendance of 1080, while Easter communions numbered 915. In his seventeen years in the parish, Watts-Ditchfield presented 1509 candidates for Confirmation, half of whom were over twenty. They were divided almost equally between men and women. [18]

Watts-Ditchfield's Politics

Watts-Ditchfield was a determined social reformer. In his sermons preached outside St. James-the-Less he repeatedly condemned the extravagance of contemporary upper and middle class life. [19] At Cambridge in 1909 he said, "We read . . . of a dozen persons sitting down to dine at a cost of five thousand pounds. All this, be it remembered, is taking place in a city overcrowded, and the people underfed, badly clothed, and largely unemployed." The next year at the Abbey he declared, "The annual income of this kingdom is about 1,700 millions, half of which is received by 5 millions of people, while the remaining 38 millions take the other half. Is this a fair distribution?" From the meagre remaining evidence, it would seem that Watts-Ditchfield preached within his own parish most frequently upon Christian doctrine and upon that "trinity of sins" of modern life, "drink, gambling, and impurity." [20] But when speaking from a national pulpit, he used the occasion to appeal for a more equitable distribution of Britain's wealth. Repeatedly he protested against Christian individualism, arguing that ". . . the principles of righteousness be applied not merely in private life but in municipal and national life . . ." as well. Using the analogy of an army, he maintained that once a person had joined the Church, his personal desires had to give way before the needs of the group as a whole. "The Christian," Watts-Ditchfield said in 1910, "is compelled to be a social reformer. He is bound to pull down the slums and see that the conditions are just and right as between man and man and between God and man." [21]

Watts-Ditchfield's political stance was rooted in the center of his theology, the fact of the Incarnation. Christ had come, he said, not to be the Savior "of the English only but of the alien, the anarchist", the dispossessed. [22] This meant that the Christian must follow his Lord in devoting himself not merely to religious works, but to every form of social improvement:

> His [Christ's] recorded life was largely concerned with the material and physical improvement of man, for His miracles, almost entirely, tended in that direction. His words as judge (St. Matt. xxv) take cognisance only of what would today be called "social work", and strangely enough, omit all reference to what we are accustomed to regard as purely spiritual needs of men. The Incarnation linked man and God together, and raised man to a platform on which he ought to have every opportunity to develop the highest that is in him. [23]

There was little place for individualism in this evangelical's piety.

Yet Watts-Ditchfield was not a socialist. In his youth he had been a Liberal and had worked earnestly for the election of Gladstone, his "favourite English statesman, past or present." [24] He watched the rise of the Labour Party sympathetically, but never committed himself to its program. Instead, he viewed Labour as "at once a rebuke and a challenge, not only to the great historical political parties which during the past century have governed England, but also to the Christian Church." Had the Church fulfilled its obligation to shape a just society, a political party which looked for support from a single social class would never have been necessary. However, he remained on good terms with the socialists. Frequently he protested against the tendency to link socialism with either infidelity or subversion of English home life, maintaining that "Some of the finest types of Christians in the East End are Socialists . . . ." [25]

Early in his tenure at St. James-the-Less, Watts-Ditchfield had argued that the Church should "in no way whatever be committed to any political party." [26] Yet he campaigned for Liberal candidates in Bethnal Green, and he became active in local politics, standing for election to the Board of Guardians that administered the Poor Law in the district. He was elected by a large majority in 1899 and served until after his consecration as Bishop. Similarly, he took occasional stands on political issues that affected the East End. During the unemployment crisis of 1908, for example, he wrote to the *Church Family Newspaper* in support of government relief. Acknowledging the demoralizing influence that indiscriminate relief often had, he argued that the danger "seems to me a small matter in comparison with the worst effects of unemployment." [27] In fact, he never agreed with the Barnetts' opposition to all forms of out-relief. Throughout his time at Bethnal Green, one curate was always on duty at the Church to deal with requests for emergency funds. [28]

Probably his most successful political foray was not directly political at all. In 1902 Watts-Ditchfield conceived that a local display of "home" industries might focus public attention on this form of exploiting East End labor. It was a common practice for businessmen to contract with individuals for the manufacture of such products as men's shirts, artificial flowers, match boxes, and paper bags. The manufacturers, who often had to supply some of their own materials, were then paid only a small fraction of the article's selling price, sometimes as little as two to three percent. The success of this venture encouraged Watts-Ditchfield to plan a much larger exhibition at St. James-the-Less in 1904. This time the show was covered by all the London newspapers, and the resulting publicity led the *Daily News* to sponsor an even larger exhibition at Queen's Hall in the West End two years later. Watts-Ditchfield opened the 1906 exhibition with a speech concluded with an appeal from Ruskin:

> Ruskin in one of his finest passages said that whenever a
> murder was committed in any community he would im-
> mediately call together the heads of the different house-
> holds, and make them draw lots to decide which of them

should be hanged. What Ruskin meant was that the
whole community was responsible for what was going on
in its midst. That exhibition, he hoped, would help to
rouse London to a sense of its responsibily to the sweated
and overcrowded people in its midst. Once get public
opinion roused, and statesmen would soon find a way by
which the evils of sweating could be got rid of and the
poor enabled to live in homes comfortable, decent, and
happy. [29]

Some relief was to come by 1912, with the creation of several Trades
Boards and the lobbying efforts of the National Anti-Sweating League.

Perhaps most important of all, Watts-Ditchfield was a zealous
democrat. Continually he condemned the control of political power by
the upper and middle classes to the detriment of the workingman. His
condemnation extended to the Church. It would be well, he argued, to
adopt the New Testament standard of qualification for ordination: "men
filled with the Holy Ghost." If this were so, workingmen would not be
relegated only to subsidiary offices in the Church's organization. "All,
even the highest posts would be open to them . . . The way working
men are **ignored** and passed over for the possessors of wealth and position is a great hindrance to ever reaching men in large masses." [30]
Watts-Ditchfield attempted to follow this principle in organizing the
Men's Club; its directors were elected by the congregation at the Men's
Service. But inevitably, none of the co-workers on his staff fulfilled the
same standard, for all were clergymen or lady workers who came from the
West End. Not until sixty years later--with the ordination at St. James-
the-Less of four workingmen as "supplementary ministers"--were Watts-
Ditchfield's professed intentions fulfilled. [31]

Watts-Ditchfield's Evangelicalism

Watts-Ditchfield was neither an original nor a particularly con-
sistent thinker. His genius lay elsewhere: in his eirenic nature, in his
effect upon men, in his talent for parochial organization. He did not
write nor did he preach in a theological vein. Thus it is impossible ade-
quately to reconstruct the theology that lay behind his achievement at St.
James-the-Less. Raymond Blathwayt, a reporter who visited the parish

in 1904, reflects the problem:

> The vicar ascended the pulpit [at the Men's Service] and
> gave an address on the relations between the sexes. He
> was certainly earnest in delivery, but I am bound to add
> the sermon itself contained no originality of thought, no
> very glowing inspiration to the higher life, though it fre-
> quently made the audience laugh audibly. But the fact re-
> mains that it was one of the largest, one of the most at-
> tentive congregations I had ever seen, with apparently
> every desirable element present except, so far as I could
> discern, that of spirituality. [32]

Yet Watts-Ditchfield considered himself, and was universally viewed by
others, as a decided evangelical. He was a supporter of the three major
evangelical associations, the Church Missionary Society, the Church
Pastoral Aid Society, and the Islington Clerical Meeting, in all of which
Champneys had been active fifty years earlier. And, at least early in his
tenure at Bethnal Green, he engaged in various skirmishes with the local
anglo-catholic clergy. Details of these difficulties have not been recorded,
but his daughter recalls that Watts-Ditchfield had few contacts with
neighboring vicars. "We opted out of the ruridecanal social scene", she
says, "because most of the members of the deanery were anglo-
catholics."

Watts-Ditchfield showed many of the outward marks of the evangelical Anglican. At Bethnal Green he always celebrated the communion service at the north end of the altar, vested in surplice and scarf. Only
at the end of his life, and then at the insistent urging of his son-in-law,
did he agree to wear a stole. He consistently referred to the anglo-
catholics as "neo-Anglicans", preached the necessity of conversion, and
spoke of Church members as having been "saved". He insisted that the
eucharistic elements of bread and wine only represented the body and
blood of Christ and urged the universal adoption of evening communions, at which he used "unfermented wine" in order not to seduce the reformed drunkards. [33] These circumstances, together with his proclivity
for Sankey hymns and open-air preaching, marked him as that rare figure
in the East End, an evangelical vicar. And yet, he was an evangelical
with a difference. No fundamentalist, he occasionally used some elemen-
tary higher criticism to help his congregation deal with obvious biblical

contradictions. And constantly he protested against the individualism of much evangelical preaching. "Justification by faith is a good beginning", he wrote in 1910, "but it must end in pulling down the slums and removing temptation from the drunkard, or it is not the doctrine according to the word of God." [34]

He was also an evangelical who changed during his seventeen years at Bethnal Green. His daughter concludes, "When he went to Bethnal Green he was a determined evangelical and was opposed to high church practices . . . He was still a very decided evangelical, but not quite so determined perhaps, when he became Bishop." She locates the period of his greatest change in 1912, during his eight-month service as a missioner to Australia and New Zealand for the Church of England Men's Society. Here, for the first time, he worked closely with anglo-catholic clergy. "The trip mellowed his attitude to high churchmen," his daughter recalls.

And yet there were earlier signs that Watts-Ditchfield was no ordinary evangelical. He did not fear the externals of worship. Immediately upon coming to St. James-the-Less, he rebuilt the chancel, dignifying the place of the altar. "An alabaster retable had been let into the wall above the altar, and over this were four mosaics representing the emblems of the evangelists, whilst three new stained-glass windows were to be seen in the apse of the sanctuary." [35] A photograph now in the possession of his family shows the same altar vested with a frontal and flanked by two large candelabra. Similarly, when Watts-Ditchfield celebrated the communion in a parishioner's home, he always insisted upon fitting up a makeshift altar in order to give dignity to the sacrament. [36] Perhaps most surprising, he was given a title by his co-workers in Bethnal Green; they always referred to him as "Daddy." [37] The connotations of the anglo-catholic "Father" are perhaps not so very different from those of this evangelical's appellation.

But the clearest evidence of his theological movement comes from his 1911 and 1913 books. In these volumes he rarely cited the Reformation divines; rather, he pointed to figures of the early Church and the Caroline period, and he advised his listeners to read such contemporary writers as Gore and Pusey and even Newman. To the divinity students at Cambridge he declared, "every Minister should know and value such works as: Augustine's **Confessions**, Bishop Andrewes' **Devotions**, Jeremy Taylor's **Holy Living and Dying**, and Law's **Serious Call**. Beyond these, I should be loathe to advise . . . . " An anglo-catholic would have been delighted with just such a list, as he would have been delighted with Watts-Ditchfield's increasingly high estimation of the communion service. Again to the Cambridge divinity students, the evangelical vicar said, ". . . I press upon you the incalculable benefits obtainable by the regular and faithful reception of . . . the Holy Communion." [38] Another time he argued against predestination, permitted prayers for the dead, and set forth a much mitigated doctrine of hell. Though he denied the terms, he came rather close to espousing a belief in both purgatory and Universalism. [39] With considerable justice the *Guardian's* review of **Here and Hereafter** included the following assessment; "Mr-Watts-Ditchfield would probably be taken as a typical and much-respected leader of the younger Evangelicals . . . Plainly, the preacher has learned much from Broad Churchmen and High Churchmen . . . He has retained all that is best in Evangelicalism and has lost its narrowness." [40]

Predictably, Watts-Ditchfield was to become less narrow as a Bishop, for he was forced to administer a diocese containing a large number of anglo-catholic clergy. The new Bishop refused to wear the cope and mitre presented to him by the anglo-catholic clergy of Chelmsford, but in more important ways he strove for comprehensiveness. In 1916, during the National Mission of Repentance and Hope, he discovered the religious retreat, until then an almost exclusively anglo-catholic practice. From then until his death, he incorporated regular clerical retreats into the life of his diocese. In 1917 he and the anglo-catholic Bishop Gore published a book on reservation of the sacrament, attempting to mediate the thorniest issue in Prayer Book reform. [41] In 1920, as President of the Church Congress, he called for the unity of anglo-catholics and evangelicals as the first priority of the Church. [42] And shortly before his death in 1923 he wrote a long letter to the *Times* in which he supported reforms of the Prayer Book and the ecclesiastical courts as the solutions to a divided Church of England:

> Between the two great parties, Evangelicals and Anglo-Catholics, there is the larger body of Church-people not openly identified with either, but simply loyal Anglicans eager and anxious to fulfill their task in peace. . . I believe the overwhelming majority of the clergy desire ardently a real attempt at a settlement of our outstanding difficulties, which, while generous and comprehensive,

would be loyal to the fundamental principles of the Reformation.

He concluded the letter in eirenic fashion: "I am encouraged to write this letter, for I believe that I am the spokesman of tens of thousands of Christian folk found in every section of the Church who say: 'We be brethren, let us meet at the feet of Him whom we all equally call our Lord and our God, and let Him tell what He would have us do.'" [43]

The Moral Influence of Top Hats

The influence of any parish at a particular time is difficult to measure. Especially is this so when the time is long past and the adult parishioners have all died. What survives are the attendance figures, and these would indicate that St. James-the-Less under Watts-Ditchfield was the most influential parish of that period in the East End. The *Daily News* statistics for 1902-03, gathered early in Watts-Ditchfield's Bethnal Green career, show that St. James-the-Less had by far the largest congregation of any parish church in the Boroughs of Stepney, Shoreditch, and Bethnal Green. [44] A recent Vicar has concluded that St. James-the-Less is "one of only two or three traditionally evangelical churches which in the past made any real impression in this part of London." [45]

And yet the question remains: impression upon whom? For it seems that those who attended St. James-the-Less were not representative of the Bethnal Green poor. After his revealing foray into the parish. Blathwayt wrote:

> He [Watts-Ditchfield] certainly has done a wonderful work when one comes to think of what the parish of St. James was when he went there seven short years ago. A top hat was hardly known, a smart bonnet was a rarity in the whole vast neighborhood; and yet Sunday to-day in that far-reaching wilderness is black with the one, it is like a flower-bed with the other. You smile, but you do not realize the significance of the change. A top hat or a pretty bonnet in Bethnal Green is more often than not-- and I say it with all reverence--the outward and visible sign of an inward spiritual grace. It is the hall mark of a changed life. It is the one infallible sign that drink, loaf-

> ing, wife-beating, stealing, swearing, and gambling have
> been for ever cast aside, and that the wearer has started on
> the heavenward way. It means everything. [46]

Apparently it did mean everything, not only to one patronizing reporter but also to those who attended the Men's Service, for another outsider in the same year observed, "The ambition, so it is further reported, with which a man is fired on coming into the church for the first time, perhaps with a cotton handkerchief tied round his neck, is to emulate his companions, and save up for a silk hat." [47] A top hat, in this district where a cloth cap was the seldom-removed and never-doffed emblem of manhood, had become the sign of the true churchman.

It would be altogether too easy to use this knowledge to ridicule Watts-Ditchfield. His service to the poor of the parish is undoubted. The depth of both his influence on them and his concern for them was genuine. That he worked in a time when people naturally associated middle-class dress with churchgoing was not his responsibility. But he largely agreed with those views. Of the Men's Service at St. Peter's he wrote: "Nothing strikes a visitor more at our service than the respectable class of men. But when a man receives Christ as his Saviour it very soon alters his appearance. Among other blessings, religion brings a man very soon a Sunday suit of black, and is aided by the help afforded by the Thrift Club." [48] The conclusion is clear. Despite all his statements to the contrary, Christianity for Watts-Ditchfield coheres with the "respectable class" of men and women. Evangelizing the poor means more than bringing the gospel to them and bringing them to the church. It means raising their social status, bringing their lives ever closer to the norms of the middle class. And it means, as a corollary, that the influence of St. James-the-Less did not fall equally across the social spectrum. The church appealed to, and drew to its services, those of the poor who were not satisfied with their social lot, those who aspired to a higher status, those who were not put off by the Cockney prejudice against trying to make oneself "a cut above the rest".

The church also appealed to some from the middle-class who lived across Victoria Park in the newly developed Hackney suburbs. It seems probable that the congregation at St. James-the-Less was drawn both from them and from the uppermost segment of the working people in Bethnal Green. The others, the truly poor working people, those who could not aspire to top hats and higher status, attended--when they went

to church at all--the Sidney Street Mission. Beyond the ostensible pur-
pose of providing a nearer place of worship for many in the parish, the
Mission must also have been founded with the recognition that St.
James-the-Less would draw its congregation from the elite of the Bethnal
Green population.

There are hints of this social division in Watts-Ditchfield's biography. Gowing writes of the newly-constructed churchyard and gardens:
"It was an impressive scene on a summer evening, when both [tennis]
courts were in use, and young folk in summer attire strolled round the
ground, or rested on the seats awaiting their turn to play tennis, whilst
cricket practice was in full swing at the nets, giving healthy exercise to a
score or more of young men." [49] Even allowing for Gowing's tendency to hyperbole, this is not a believable scene in which the average
young man of Bethnal Green might participate. Again, of the farewell reception for Watts-Ditchfield after he was made Bishop, Gowing writes:
"Men and women, young and old, were there; people from the poorest
parts of the parish, and those more intimately associated with the
Church, were seated side by side." [50] Gowing's unconscious dichoto-
my between the poor and the churchmen is the best evidence that, though
St. James-the-Less served the poor, it drew its main congregation from
elsewhere.

About 1960, when the Vicar asked one of his oldest ladies
about the parish at the beginning of the century, she replied: "Oh, I never went to church. The church wasn't for the likes of me, we all went to
the Mission." The Vicar concluded, "By tacit agreement, attendance in
church was for the better class of people, who came across Victoria park
from South Hackney, and who were gentry. They lived in the four storey
villas, now converted into three flats each, and their servants went to the
Mission." [51] This is surely over-stated; Bethnal Green working people
did come to St. James-the-Less and formed a large part of the congregation at the Men's Service. [52] But it does point in the right direction.
The congregations at St. James-the-Less were not nearly as representative
of Bethnal Green as were those at the Sidney Street Mission. And though
Watts-Ditchfield was justly famed in his day for service to the poor, the
size of his congregations provides an inadequate index of his influence
upon the average residents of Bethnal Green.

Watts-Ditchfield: An Assessment

Watts-Ditchfield today has been unfairly forgotten. He is
mentioned once in Roger Lloyd's **The Church of England 1900-
1965**, not at all in Owen Chadwick's **The Victorian Church**, and
only in passing by the various historians of evangelical Anglicanism.
Yet he was, in the numbers of people he attracted to church, the most
successful East End clergyman of his own time, Once turned down by
the Wesleyans for missionary service abroad, he conceived himself a missionary within London. And this he managed to be, with a less patronizing spirit than that of either Lowder or Barnett, for he was not a university man, and in some degree he was only a generation removed from the
social class of his parishioners. His father, after all, had gone into the
factory at the age of eight. His dedication was legendary. He would respond to sick calls at any hour. Often he took drunkards into his own
home and successfully helped them overcome their addiction. He was, in
short, a model parish priest, one who could rightfully be remembered in
any list of modern Anglican saints.

Yet his greatest achievement was probably outside the parish.
He tried to form a new school of evangelicalism, one tied neither to a
Tory past nor to reaction against the anglo-catholics. Inglis has written:
". . . it was evangelicalism, not Nonconformity, that offered a peculiar
resistance to social radicalism. The sternest Christian opponents of reform were those who believed most completely that body and soul were
antithetical, and that the duty of a Christian was to reject the world, not
to sanctify it." [53] In large measure, Inglis is undoubtedly correct. But
Watts-Ditchfield was more than a glorious exception; he had a precursor
in Champneys, and he has successors (albeit ones ignorant of his contribution) in the modern evangelical movement. Today, the most vital parish churches in East London are, almost without exception, those that are
evangelical.

The changing nature of evangelicalism in nineteenth century
England has never received sufficient attention. No one would confuse a
Charles Lowder with a spokesman for the Oxford Movement in 1840,
much less with an earlier high churchman who looked back nostalgically
to the Carolines and the non-Jurors. Few exist who could not distinguish
between a latitudinarian of the eighteenth century and a broad churchman,
informed by Maurice, a hundred years later. And yet, a similar movement on the part of evangelicals is often ignored by church historians.

Alexander Zabriskie has shown clearly that until the middle of the nineteenth century the evangelicals remained distinct from the mostly Tory low churchmen, and that it was only in reaction to the development of ritualism and to the 1860 publication of *Essays and Reviews* that an alliance between evangelicalism, theological obscurantism, and political conservatism was forged. [54] Despite this clear evidence, however, nineteenth century evangelicalism is still too often viewed as a single, monolithic phenomenon. Such a view obscures the development of a new evangelical party at the end of the century, one that tended to be just as incarnational in its theology, just as socially progressive, and just as distinguished by parochial service, as the broad church or anglo-catholic movement. The party may have been small, but by his elevation to Chelmsford Watts-Ditchfield gave it an imprimatur.

It would be easy, from the perspective lent by a distance of seventy-five years, to debunk Watts-Ditchfield's achievement at St. James-the-Less. Often he pandered to his congregation, leading them to laughter rather than conversion. He tolerated and even fostered the social division of his parish into church and mission. And he failed to carry out the radical political implications of his theology, cherishing instead a sentimental fondness for the church-going Liberals of the preceding generation. He, to a greater extent than his father before him, had become a gentleman and he expected his parishioners to do the same. Little wonder that he was tempted to regard the acquisition of a top hat as evidence of moral reformation.

But despite this criticism, he accomplished what few others, before or after him, have been able to do. He created a bridge between the classes, albeit one with many planks missing, a bridge over which some of his parishioners were able to climb toward social respectability and a more secure life. And to those who could not or would not climb, he nevertheless gave his attention and zeal. He publicized their plight and tried--in the small ways that good parish priests have always tried--to bring them acceptance and hope. Few of his time labored more earnestly in the East End. None more honestly earned the admiration of his people.

V

THE EAST LONDON GENTLEMEN

The East End slums were not the worst examples of nine-teenth century urban poverty. Those were to be found abroad, as often as not in the British colonies. Even within London itself, some of the most horrible instances of deprivation could be seen in the West End, high-lighted by their proximity to the wealth of the world's most industrialized nation. But if the East End slums were not in fact unique, they nonethe-less gained a pre-eminence over other blighted areas in and even beyond England. By the middle of Victoria's reign, the East End had become sy-nonymous with, and the symbolic of, that unwanted step-child of the in-dustrial revolution, the proletarian dregs, the impoverished masses created by the new order. The urban slums had roots that stretched back at least a hundred years, but not until the early nineteenth century were they rec-ognized as a new phenomenon. From then on, from Victoria's accession until well after the First World War, the slum became a major focus for social planners, politicians, educators, churchmen, and the dispensers of charity. For good reasons the middle class feared the slum--it was not only an affront to their vision of an affluent society, but it was also a continuing menace to their social and economic position. The slum-dwellers embodied the threat of revolution. Yet fear was not the sole reaction engendered by the East End, for that enigmatic area exerted a myriad of fascinations similar to those of the most distant colonies, while it elicited also a decent measure of sympathy and concern. The Vic-torians, after all, should be remembered for their liberality as well as for their exploitation and their prudery.

The slum was perhaps the greatest challenge to Victorian England's inherited institutions. The reaction of the church would be crit-ical. Working with the preconceptions of parochial organization appro-priate to village life, the church suddenly found itself confronted by un-

churched masses, just as alienated from formal religion as they were
from industrial prosperity. The Church of England had little in its history to guide its approach to the slum, for evangelism has never been the
strength of an established denomination. Working from the only model it
knew, the foreign mission field, the Church of England's publications became increasingly filled with calls to "home missions", to the Chris-
tianization of masses who were distinguished by their contiguousness
with the nation that produced the missionaries. One such article reiterat-
ed the constant theme: "The greatest problem before our Church today is
how to evangelize the crowded centres of population." [1] The home
mission was a new reality, one that would test both the flexibili-
ty of the Church of England's institutions, and ultimately the reality
of its establishment.

The Church of England in the Victorian East End presents a
confusing and often conflicting picture. There was no central conception
guiding its work, no clear vision of what had to be done. Bishop Blomfield had responded in the only way he knew--by building more churches
and by creating more parishes. But these did not define the character of
the church's efforts in the area. All they did was to provide more arenas
where individual clergymen and their small staffs could work out new
patterns of ministry. Every party in the church--not just the anglo-
catholics, as is so often thought--became active in the field. Writing toward the end of the century, James Adderley surveyed the parishes of the
East End:

> Church work is very vigorous in many places with vari-
> ous methods. Advanced ritualism, with untiring, self-
> denying work for 40 years at St. Peter's, London Docks;
> steady Anglicanism, with sympathetic social reformation
> work at Poplar and Stepney parish churches; earnest,
> homely Evangelicalism at St. Mary's, Whitechapel;
> honest, plodding labour on good Bible and Prayer-book
> lines at St. Andrew's, Bethnal Green, and All Hallows,
> East India Docks--these are some of the churches which
> I have come across and learnt to admire. [2]

What those clergymen did, and the kinds of ministry they developed,
have been the focus of this study.

This study has been divided along the lines of the three major church parties, because those divisions were the dominant reality of the Victorian Church of England. It has concentrated on three outstanding examples--Lowder, Barnett, and Watts-Ditchfield--who were judged by their contemporaries to be the most successful East End clergy representing each of those parties. But it has focused on these men also because they have left behind more extensive records of their parochial work than any of their fellow clergymen in the East End. They all wrote about their experiences in the slums. Between 1837 and 1914 perhaps one thousand clergymen spent considerable portions of their ministries in the East End. Among these undoubtedly were a host of unremembered saints, perhaps as well a few geniuses of parochial organization whose methods were never noticed. But most of these now lie beyond the grasp of modern historians. What few documents they did bequeath have all too often been lost by later neglect or destroyed by German bombs. A complete history of the Church of England in the Victorian East End is an impossibility. All that remain are bits and pieces for the historian to fit together into a picture that he can hope to be representative.

The third series of Charles Booth's **Life and Labour** presented a sequence of vignettes that testified to the vitality of East End church work at the close of Victoria's reign. Its three-page summary of St. Dunstan's, for example, is typical except for the size of the parish and the extent of its organizations:

> The most marked feature of the work of the Church of England here [the East End] is the extensive scale of which, in many instances, it is carried on. We have, for instance, the mother parish of Stepney, St. Dunstan's, with a population of 22,000. It can boast two churches, two schools, three mission-rooms, a parish room and four halls. Besides the rector there are five curates, two Scripture readers and seven paid lady workers, together with about 150 voluntary workers and a corresponding list of activities. [3]

Walter Besant--who, like Booth, was no admirer of the Established Church--confirmed this picture: "The clergy [of the East End], with or without this magnetic power, work day and night. Never before has the Church of England possessed a clergy more devoted to practical work." [4] But these are only very partial impressions. What is lacking in Booth is any comprehensive view of how particular clergy and their staffs went about their parochial labors.

There is little to fill this gap but the testimony of the slum clergy themselves, and these recollections present the historian with all the problems of self-serving declarations. Fortunately there are a few exceptions. When Besant visited one of the least noted East End parishes, St. James', Ratcliff, he was amazed by what he found. [5] Because the area was one of the most depressed in all London, and because the church was unknown for any active work among the poor, he had expected to discover an indolent vicar ignoring the dreadful conditions around him. Besant had little regard for the church as an institution, but he did hope that its clergy might serve to uplift the poor in small ways, for ". . . without the presence among a people of some higher life, some nobler standard, than that of the senses, this people will sink rapidly and surely". What he found, to his great surprise, were three faithful clergymen working alongside a large staff of volunteers. Daily services were being held, and although the average Sunday attendance was only about three hundred, more than that number were involved in the Sunday schools and bible classes. The clergy had transformed the churchyard into a recreation ground and had rented a nearby building as a gymnasium, where they promoted five athletic teams for the neighborhood boys. An adjacent building had been designated the "Mission Chapel" to house at least a dozen more parish organizations. A children's play room and a men's club were open every evening. Each week the parish sponsored a dramatic performance, a concert, a gymnastic display, and a lecture. Classes in nursing, carpentry, singing, and shorthand were held. Finally, a savings bank, a sick and distress fund, a library, a country holiday fund, and a weekly second-hand clothing sale were maintained. All this cost nearly a thousand pounds a year and involved a large staff: "The whole number of men and women engaged in organizing work connected with the Church is about 126." The clergy and the volunteers were "the only gentlefolk . . . working in the parish." And yet the church was, according to Besant, "the least known of Riverside London." He concluded: "When we remenber that Ratcliff is not what is called a "show" parish, that the newspapers never talk about it, and that rich people never hear of it, this indicates a very considerable support to Church work." [6] Besant's description indicates much more than the vitality of the church's efforts in the East End. It suggests also how few of those efforts were recorded for the benefit of future historians, for without his account, St. James' would be wholly unremembered today. There must have been dozens of similar parishes, staffed by hundreds of clergy and volunteers, that have passed with even less notice.

Churchmanship and the East End: A Comparison

The evidence that does remain of the church in the Victorian East End consists very largely of highlights from a general picture of clerical energy and enthusiasm. But even that evidence often does not give a clear view of a particular clergyman's parochial thinking. This is especially true in the case of Charles Lowder, whose habitual reserve prevented all but a modicum of self-revelation in his writings. The outward facts of Lowder's ministry are clear. His attitude toward his parishioners, however, and even his manner of teaching them remain obscure. Similarly, it would be interesting to know Samuel Barnett's minimal standard for a profession of Christian faith. Toynbee Hall was obviously, at least in its origins, an extension of his parochial work. But whether he considered the settlement in any way a substitute for the parish, or whether he thought its educational program a necessary prerequisite to faith, is ambiguous. Likewise, it is unclear whether James Watts-Ditchfield consciously divided his parish into church and chapel. If he did so, it might be unfair to consider him a slum clergyman at all. But it seems nore likely that the division arose gradually, as much a result of the congregation's attitudes as of his own choice. Despite these uncertainties, however, it is possible to compare their parochial ministries and to draw some conclusions regarding the relative importance of their varying schools of churchmanship.

The most striking conclusion that arises from this comparison concerns the similarity of their approaches to the parish. In large measure they all accepted the traditional methods of such work: house-to-house visitation, frequent church services, an emphasis on religious instruction, and great attention to the children, particularly by the construction and support of parish schools. It was a model of the parochial ministry that George Herbert or Richard Baxter would instantly have recognized. Despite their missionary stance, despite their conviction that they were pioneering a new approach to the slum, all three fell back on the most traditional pattern of parish ministry, one that had its roots in catholicism, but one that came to them most directly from the reformed churches. Even Lowder, who consciously patterned his ministry after

that of Vincent de Paul, did not diverge significantly from the reformed
ideal. His stress on house-to-house visiting and on constant catechesis
owed at least as much to his protestant background as to his catholic convictions. He intended to found a religious order, but he succeeded merely
in becoming a model pastor.

Perhaps the most striking similarity between the three--
striking because it is so unexpected--is that they all indulged in liturgical
illegalities. All three, not just the anglo-catholic Lowder, found the
Book of Common Prayer an inadequate vehicle for the worship of their
slum congregations. In large measure, the faith of the Anglican middle
classes was focused on the Prayer Book; they were, above all, a people of
the written word. But the printed book carried much less authority in the
East End, where as many as half the people in the poorest districts might be functional illiterates. The successful East End clergymen,
despite their litany of praise for the normal worship of the Established
Church, all looked to other sources for ways to make their services speak
to their people. Lowder, of course, drew so many "enrichments" from the
Roman Missal that his eucharists were more like the Roman mass than
an Anglican communion. Barnett and Watts-Ditchfield, on the other
hand, looked to the worship of the Nonconformist churches. The bish-
ops were not entirely happy with either the Worship Hour or the Men's
Service, so clearly modeled on non-Anglican sources, but they did not in-
terfere. After permitting, however grudgingly, the liturgical irregularities
of the anglo-catholics, they would have been in a poor position to ban
similar innovations on the part of broad churchmen or evangelicals. The
Worship Hour became the popular service at St. Jude's, just as the Men's
Service did at St. James-the-Less. The Prayer book remained a vehicle for
the clergy's private devotions, but it lost ground as the normal means of
public worship.

The East End clergy looked to different sources for the
Prayer Book's enrichment or replacement, but at the most fundamental level their additions all tended in the same directions--they
aimed at brightening their services with music and art, with color and
light and enthusiasm. The anglo-catholics alone have been termed ritualists. But in a real sense, the successful broad churchmen and evangelicals were ritualists, as well. They were all concerned with reforming
worship so that it might be more involving and understandable to their
slum congregations.   They all wanted to attract the poor. Perhaps the
difference between Lowder's Gregorian chant and Barnett's oratorios and

Watt's-Ditchfield's Sankey hymns is less significant than the fact of their joint introduction into staid Anglican worship. All were attempts to make the Church of England appealing to unchurched East Enders who had no familiarity with, and little aptitude for, the Book of Common Prayer.

There is another important, and more obvious, similarity between these parishes. All dispensed with any distinction between "spiritual" and "secular" ministries, each attempting on a broad front to attack the problems of the slums and to raise the standard of their parishioners' lives. To this end, all developed large staffs of both clergy and lay volunteers who worked together to provide a level of education, cultural enrichment, social opportunities, vocational training, and poor relief ordinarily denied to slum dwellers. All in large measure fit Besant's description of the model East End parish:

> There are the services of the parish church, with outly-
> ing mission churches; there are Sunday-schools, there are
> clubs, there are mothers' meetings, there are amusements
> for the people--concerts and entertainments for the win-
> ter; there is the supervision of the visiting ladies who go
> about the parish and learn the history of all the tenants in
> all the courts. There is the choir to be looked after, there
> are the sick to be cared for, there are always people in dis-
> tress and in need of help--people for whom the vestry offi-
> cers and workhouse officers can do nothing; the despairing
> young clergyman very soon finds out that the more you
> give to people who want help, the more people there are
> who clamor for help. [7]

Besant, of course, continued by expressing his fear that the clergy were pauperizing their people by inuring them to the dole rather than to self-improvement. But Barnett and the other broad churchmen--most of whom were identified with the Charity Organization Society--were the only clergy who openly shared this worry. Lowder and Watts-Ditchfield constantly provided relief, as Barnett himself increasingly did after he broke with the dogmatism of the C.O.S.

The more important point is that all three eventually rejected any narrow view of the clergy's role and attempted to make their churches into community centers, alternatives to both the streets and the public houses. Lowder always had reservations about assuming such a secular role, initially leaving all relief work to the sisters. But as the sisters withdrew from the parish, and as Linklater developed his St. Agatha's mission, he was increasingly forced to accept a much broader model of the ministry than the one with which he had begun. During Wainright's time, St. Peter's became noted for its active club life. By the end of the century, then, a consensus about the form of a successful East End parish had arisen from the efforts by churchmen of every theological persuasion: such a parish had a large staff, held many and colorful church services, and sponsored a large variety of social clubs, athletic teams, entertainments, and relief efforts. With a few exceptions, such as St. Jude's and St. James', Ratcliff, participation in these secular activities was tied to church attendance. The church, after all, had its *raison d'etre* in the worship of God.

It has frequently been said that service in the slums radicalized ministers, that the East End clergy were notable for their political activities and, as the nineteenth century came to a close, for their socialism. But this seems to have been true of only a very small segment of such clergymen. Septimus Hansard was a socialist in the Maurician mold long before he went to Bethnal Green. Barnett proclaimed himself a "practicable socialist" as a result of his experiences in Whitechapel, but this fuzzy appellation was translated into little more than art exhibitions.

Of the period's three flamboyant "Christian socialists" so often cited--Robert Dolling, Arthur Stanton, and Stewart Headlam--none spent any significant portion of his ministry in the East End. There have been many attempts to claim for the anglo-catholics, especially for Lowder and Mackonochie, an effective opposition to sweated industries, but such claims seem more clearly based in hagiography than in history. In general, the East End clergy were remarkably apolitical. Few were Tory conservatives, most were at least vaguely liberal, but all seemed to sense that direct political action lay outside the province of a parish clergyman.

None of the East End ministries considered here was typical, if by that is meant a parish that inspired a great many imitators. Each was considered in its day a model of what a clergyman of a particular party might do with a slum church. Each became a training-ground for curates, most of whom went on to ministries outside the slums. Strangely, no other East End parishes seemed to pattern themselves on these models. The exception, if indeed it is one, existed on the level of the ideal rather than the actual. The ministry at St. Peter's became a paradigm for many anglo-catholics, often invoked but rarely followed. The parish's influence

even extended beyond the ritualists. In 1892, after a discussion that had
lasted for three years, the Canterbury Convocation finally adopted a report
reconnending that slum ministries be carried on by "brotherhoods of clergy" whose members would be bound by temporary vows of celibacy. [8]
It was a remarkable and ironic recommendation, for it showed the extent
to which Lowder's ideal had triumphed in theory even though he had never been able to make a lasting college of clergy work in practice. The
fascination with this particular pattern of slum ministry has continued
among later historians. Lowder is a justly famous figure, but he has been
made famous at the expense of broad churchmen and evangelicals who
carried on equally effective work in the East End. And that fame has
tended also to obscure the very real similarities between Lowder's ministry and those of other East End clergymen who shared his commitment
to the slums but not his theological position.

 Since St. Peter's, St. Jude's, and St. James-the-Less were all
noted for their individualistic ministries, it is significant that none was
one of the East End's older churches. All three were "district parishes"
dating from the middle of the nineteenth century. When Lowder, Barnett,
and Watts-Ditchfield arrived in the East End, each entered a virtually unchurched area. Thus each was free from the constraints of an existing congregation, each free to develop his own ministry in the way he chose.
That was not the case in the older parish churches, those founded before
the nineteenth century. Booth noted the difference: "The great mother parish churches hold a kind of Cathedral position. The ordinary services in
them are never extreme in character, and congregations, although no
doubt mainly middle class, contain all grades of parishioners." He con-
trasted them with the district parishes, where ". . . there is far more variety both of men and method [than] in the other churches." [9] This variety was sometimes deplored. Harry Jones, for example, once devoted
thirty-eight pages to an attack on parochial subdivision. He particularly
disliked the opportunity it gave anglo-catholics of developing an extreme
ritual.   But he also argued that the new parishes were contributing a
growing "Congregationalism" within the Church of England.   "A District Parish", he wrote, "marks a departure from one principle of a national or established Church. It has no traditional corporate vitality." The
incumbents of such parishes, he continued, were free from the restraints
under which Anglican clergy had always been expected to minister: a lay
vestry, a socially varied congregation, and local parochial traditions.
Jones went to vitriolic lengths, declaring that, "The residents in a dis-

trict are as a heap of sand, without natural coherence." But he was probably correct when he argued that ". . . the excessive entanglement of the clergy in minute semi-secular pastoral work, has been unwittingly promoted, to some extent, by the subdivision of large parishes in the poorest part of London." [10]

Jones was a good representative of the old order. A broad churchman and a supporter of the C.O.S., he believed there should be a carefully defined, "spiritual" sphere for a clergyman's activities. He protested against the often idiosyncratic ministries being developed by churchmen of all parties in the East End slums. And yet he was not in a strong position to protest. He pointed with pride to the one hundred Easter communicants at St. George's-in-the-East, most of whom were from the middle class. It was clear that the old parish churches, bound as they were to existing congregations and traditional Anglicanism, could not adopt a missionary stance toward their mostly poor parishioners. Parochial subdivision provided the opportunity for younger clergy to evolve new patterns of slum ministry. Whether those new patterns proved successful or not, the Church of England had at least attempted to meet the challenge of the slum.

The East End Gentlemen: A Final Assessment

The success of any ministry is difficult, if not impossible, to measure. If impact on the English imagination is taken as the standard of success, then Lowder was certainly the pre-eminent East End clergyman. If church attendance is the standard, then Lowder and Watts-Ditchfield were immensely successful, while Barnett lagged far behind. But surely these are inadequate measures. All three made a considerable impact on the slum communities around them; all three significantly reinterpreted the Church of England's parochial ministry to fit the new conditions of the slum. All three were generally thought to have contributed to a renaissance of the church in the East End. Perhaps that is sufficient evidence to term each a success.

Despite this evidence, however, dispassionate contemporaries tended to judge the efforts of at least their colleagues as a failure. That was true of Booth, who concluded from his study of East End churches that ". . . the general effect is that of failure. . . ." [11] Similarly, after describing the energetic work of the typical East End parish, Besant

wrote. "If, on the other hand, it is asked how far the people respond . . .
it is necessary to reply that the church, as a rule, remains comparatively
empty." [12] That was the conclusion, also, of the *Daily News* census.
Sunmarizing the survey's results for the East End, Percy Alden found that
here, as elsewhere in London, there was a negative correlation between
poverty and church attendance: "The first and most noticeable result of
our examination of the census totals is the discovery that the Anglican
Church, which is supposed to be strongest in poor districts owing to the
excellent work done by a certain section of the High Church clergy, is
not nearly as strong as expected." [13] While hostility to the clergy was
on the decline, Alden noted, that was seemingly the most positive statement one could make about the church in the East End.

     Mudie-Smith did not compare his results with those of the Re-
ligious Census of 1851, for he believed the former survey to have been
woefully unscientific. But whatever the worth of the 1851 study, a comparison between the two is revealing. Where Horace Mann found that
just under thirty percent of East End residents attended some kind of
church worship, the figure fifty years later was just under twenty percent.
[14] Despite the undoubted rise in the standard of East End clergy, despite the infusion of so much energy and idealism into East End Parishes
in the latter half of the Victorian era, the churches failed to reach the inhabitants of the slum.

     This conclusion is only reinforced by later evidence. The end
of the Victorian and the beginning of the Edwardian eras are often seen as
the high-water mark for the church in the East End. In terms of clerical
enthusiasm that was true, but such energies were soon dissipated. Even
the settlement houses, for which Besant expressed such high hopes, had
gone into decline by 1914. Writing immediately after the Second World
War, Robert Sinclair testified to the emptiness of East End churches,
contrasting it with the period of the mid-Victorian "missioner": "At the
end of eighty years his successor is ignored, the soup bowl unwanted, the
parochial commemoration tablet cracked and uncared for, the lifetime's
sacrifice forgotten, the church empty and the cinema full." [15] One
looks in vain at present-day Wapping, or Whitechapel, or Bethnal Green
for the long-range effects of a Lowder, or a Barnett, or a Watts-Ditchfield.
The recent Bishop of Stepney, Trevor Huddleston, confessed the church's
failure:

        In spite of the devotion of many great priests and mini-
        sters of the gospel who have spent their lives here, in

spite of their readiness to share as fully as possible the
hardships and the bitter poverty of the years before the
Welfare State, in spite of large investment by the Church
in buildings and staff, the Church since the Industrial
Revolution has never been the Church of the working
class. It is only if we can recognize the extent and magni-
tude of this alienation that we can appreciate the urgency
of the task.

"For whom", Sinclair asked rhetorically of the present-day East End
church, "is the fabric maintained?" [16]

The church's failure in the East End was perceived at the turn
of the century by most observers who were not blinded by enthusiasm for
particular clergymen. But their analyses of the failure varied greatly.
Some--like Besant, and to a large extent, Booth also--expressed consterna-
tion that so much good clerical work should go unrewarded by the people's response. Mudie-Smith, on the other hand, presented a list of four,
largely superficial, reasons for this lack of response: the shortage of popular preachers, dark and forbidding church buildings, the dearth of open-air
preaching, and the want of a true social gospel. But it is doubtful, even
if all these deficiencies could somehow have been corrected, that the response would have been substantially greater. Percy Alden was probably
more nearly correct when he argued that church attendance was closely
tied to social class. In poor areas like the East End, he wrote, church attendance conferred no social status, and as a consequence the people did
not come. [17] Booth reached approximately the same conclusion, arguing that only the upwardly mobile in the working classes attended
church: "Wherever the regular working-class is found, and in whatever
proportion to the rest of the inhabitants, it seems equally impervious to
the claims of religion . . . while those who do join any church become
almost indistinguishable from the class with which they then mix, the
change that has really come about is not so much of as out of the class
to which they have belonged." [18]

By the turn of the century a consensus was beginning to arise,
a consensus that the working classes, ever since the industrial revolution,
had been beyond the reach of the church. Winnington-Ingram, for example, wrote: "It is not that the Church of God has lost the great towns; it
has never had them." [19] Most modern observers, including Bishop
Wickham, have come to the same conclusion. The history of the church

in the twentieth century has included many subsequent attempts to reach
the urban workers, most notably the worker-priest movement in France
and the various industrial missions in England and in the United States.
At best, none has proved more than a limited and temporary success. One
importance of the slum missions in Victorian England is that they were
the first of these attempts. Certainly they failed in their larger purpose,
but as the first in the line of so many failures, they deserve to be viewed
sympathetically and with due credit for their small successes, however parochial or ephemeral.

In the light of these later attempts, it is difficult to isolate any
single cause for the failure of the slum missions. If the parish was not an
adequate vehicle, the settlement houses and the industrial missions--both
alternatives to the parochial ministry--were no more successful. If it was
due to the lack of a social gospel, as Mudie-Smith thought, the same
charge could not be made of the later, and equally unsuccessful, attempts
to reach the working class. It may just be that the Christian church is so
hopelessly tied to the middle and upper classes, at least in the western
world, that its attempts to reach the industrial laborers have been doomed
from the start.

However great their zeal or noble their purpose, the clergymen
who came to the East End during the Victorian era were all, in a real
sense, foreigners. They were gentlemen, almost to a man from middle-
class backgrounds, most with university educations. They were men
doubly set apart from those they sought to serve, certainly by their ordination, but perhaps more importantly by their social class. They
brought with them little understanding of their parishioners. As Barnett
observed, even the most stringent voluntary asceticism could not teach
him what it was like to be truly poor. They brought with them, as well,
expectations that their new parishioners could not possibly fulfill. The
gulf between Disraeli's two nations was awesomely great. Try as they
might, the East End gentlemen could not help but patronize their neighbors. Perhaps it is significant that in all the literature surveyed for this
study, there is not a single reference before 1970 to an East End clergyman who encouraged a parishioner to study for the ministry. The clergy
came from one world and the slum dwellers from another. The wonder
may be that so many of the slum clergy managed to close that gap at all.
But this was a problem to which the Victorians were, in large measure,
blind. Indeed, they gloried in their gentlemanly priests, believing that
the ideals of culture and religion were inextricable intertwined. The 1886

plea for "home missions" only slightly exaggerated the contemporary view:

> Lastly, the ideal mission priest must be a highly-cultured English gentleman. There is abundant room in the ministry of our Church for the man of vigorous mind or deep research, for the able preacher, or the wise administrator, but let him not carry his valuable powers into the mission field, unless he have also the address and bearing, the outward polish, that neither books nor conscious self-direction will impart. There is as much need in S. Giles-in-the-Fields, or the Isle of Dogs, of refined courtesy and gentleman-like tact as in the parishes of S. Peter's, Eaton Square, or S. James', Paddington. [20]

If there was a single, fundamental reason for the missions' failure, it was this. But at the time the difficulties of a gentleman ministering to a slum congregation were recognized by very few. One of those few was C. F. G. Masterman, who wrote that, "We come from outside with our gospel . . . aliens with alien ideas." The Church of England was not successful in the slum, he argued, precisely because it ". . . represents the ideas of the upper classes, of the universities . . . ." The Nonconformists were hardly in a better position, for their ties were to an energetic and rising middle class. "Each totally fails to apprehend a vision of life as reared in a mean street, and now confronting existence on a hazardous weekly wage, from the block dwelling . . . Our movements and inexplicable energies are received with a mixture of tolerance and perplexity." [21]

Masterman, however, was an observer of rare insight. With few exceptions, his contemporaries continued to believe that only clergy from the upper ranks of society would be able to set a proper example in the midst of a slum. Since the middle and upper classes had already fled the East End, so the Victorian reasoning went, it was doubly important that clergy sent there be gentlemen, for they would be almost the last outposts of civilized culture in that whole neglected area. If the clergy were to "raise the masses", or at least to prevent the upper stratum of the poor from falling any lower, they must embody the breeding that alone could act as a counterweight to all the forces of urban degeneracy. To many Victorians, it was more important to have a gentleman-priest in the East End than anywhere else in England.

Brian Heeney has recently argued that the "gentleman-ideal" of the clergyman very largely shaped the mid-Victorian development of a "distinct clerical character". During those years, Heeney writes, "a surge of pastoral energy and a deepening of devotion among the parochial clergy" affected every party within the Church of England, giving rise to a new idealism about the clerical office, one that emphasized its sacredness, its unique responsibilities, and its "apartness". Instead of breaking with the older tradition of the gentleman-priest, however, this new ideal merely reinforced that tradition, adopting gentility as one of the primary priestly attributes. By the later years of the Victorian era, the ideal clergyman was almost universally defined as "an educated gentleman, detached from the world and permanently committed to full-time ministry." This cohesion between the gentleman-ideal and the clerical office, Heeney believes, seriously compromised the church's ability to respond to a changing social order, particularly in the slum:

> The clergyman's sense of isolation had its origin, not in
> an absence of slum community-consciousness, but in the
> parson's own incapacity to recognize that culture. Be-
> cause of his elevated social status and his alien pattern of
> life and education, he had no part in the life-style of the
> slum community. [22]

Heeney has overstated his case, for none of the outstanding East End clergy evinced any "sense of isolation." Some, men like Lincoln Wainright, could seemingly not tolerate being anywhere else. Yet Heeney's major point is a valid one: the social distance between the slum clergy and their parishioners was often too great for either to traverse successfully.

· Yet at least the attempt was made. However quixotic or hopeless the task they had set for themselves, the clergy of the Victorian East End tried to bridge the gap between two nations. That they were so often unsuccessful should occasion no surprise. What is more notable is the tenacity and the verve they brought to their work. Even if they had failed utterly, and in at least their own parishes they did not, there would still be a dimension of nobility in their efforts. Whether one takes the view of a cynic or a hagiographer, theirs was still a remarkable ministry.

There is a perfectly legitimate cynical view, for middle-class England was increasingly terrified by the East End throughout the Victo-

rian era. The new world that had sprung up just beyond Aldgate chal-
lenged every comfortable assumption about England as a unified, evolv-
ing, and above all, Christian society. The East End represented the threat
of revolution and chaos. The Reform Bills, the Poor Law, the various
Mansion House Funds, the new social legislation, all these hardly
seemed to alleviate a steadily worsening situation. In their desperation,
many Englishmen pinned their hopes on the church. The church, after
all, had always been a primary agent of social control. The attention paid
to the church in the East End, as well as the funds and personnel channeled to it, must be viewed in this light. If the church could only attract
the upper stratum of the urban poor, providing them with discipline and
the hope of rising socially, the great mass of slum dwellers would be de-
prived of their natural leaders, and the threat of revolution might be cut
off. [23] The young and enthusiastic clergy moved to the East End to
take the place of the absent gentry, to exercise the restraining functions
normally performed by members of that class.

But while all this is true, it is only a very partial view of the
slum clergy. For the most part they were genuinely idealistic men who
could have looked forward to less demanding and more prestigious, not to
say more lucrative, careers elsewhere. They, together with the women
who worked alongside them, devoted themselves to the poor with a rare
energy and dedication. They have earned the praise of their later hagiogra-
phers. However unsympathetic one's view, they represented a great advance over many of the schemes for the East End's social betterment,
over both the harsh legalism of the C.O.S. and the fashionable slumming of the eighteen-eighties. At the very least, they succeeded in bringing friendship to countless individuals within their parishes. The slum
clergy thought of their work as saving souls. In their own terms, perhaps they did just that.

APPENDIX

CHURCHMANSHIP AND CHURCH ATTENDANCE

Collating the data from the 1902-03 *Daily News* survey of the church attendance in London (from the Mudie-Smith volume) with the list of English Parishes in *Crockford's Clerical Directory for 1903* and with the details on parochial practices in the *Tourist's Church Guide* for 1901-02, it is possible to construct at least an impressionistic test of the common hypothesis that anglo-catholic clergy were more successful than those of any other church party in attracting the East End poor. That this test is only a tentative one is due to several factors: (1) the limited number of parishes here sampled; (2) the fact that these figures do not take into account varying parish sizes; (3) the frequent discrepancies between Mudie-Smith. *Crockford's*, and the *T.C.G.*, e.g. parishes listed by Mudie-Smith that do not appear in either of the other sources; (4) the doubtful character of many of the characterizations in the *T.C.G.*, e.g. its failure to list St. James-the-Less, Bethnal Green, although the parish certainly had at least one communion service every Sunday; and (5) the fact that Mudie-Smith's figures lump together attendance at several services, making it likely that many of the parishioners have been counted twice (if they went to church both in the morning and the evening), and making it impossible to distinguish between those who went to matins and those who went to communion. With these caveats in mind, it is possible to draw some tentative conclusions regarding the relationship between churchmanship and church attendance in the two East End districts for which there is substantial agreement between the three sources: the eighteenth-century parishes of Bethnal Green (divided during the nineteenth century into fourteen parishes) and St. George's-in-the-East (divided during the nineteenth century into six parishes).

Each of these twenty parishes is rated for churchmanship on a scale of one to five:

1. No weekly celebration of the communion

2. A weekly celebration, usually with the eastward position
of the celebrant, but without candles or vestments
3. A weekly celebration with lighted altar candles
4. A weekly (and in all but one case, a daily) celebration with
lighted candles and eucharistic vestments
5. A daily celebration with candles and vestments and the use
of incense on Sundays and other festivals.

In the following table I have followed the *T.C.G.'s* subjective characterization of St. James-the-Less, Bethnal Green, as an abysmally unsacramental parish. To include it with the other churches having a weekly celebration would not reflect Watts-Ditchfield's vigorous evangelicalism. It must be remembered that these figures are valid only for the period 1902-03.

St. George's-in-the-East

Parish	Church-manship	Men	Women	Atten-dance	Total
St. George's	2	92	239	123	454
St. Matthew's	2	51	66	147	264
St. John the Evangelist	3	28	35	41	104
Christ Church	4	65	116	162	343
St. Mary's	4	66	108	119	293
St. Peter's	5	204	214	674	1092

Bethnal Green

St. Paul's	1	78	137	122	337
St. Philip's	1	51	76	111	238
St. Matthias'	1	68	91	119	278

Parish	Church-manship	Men	Women	Atten-dance	Total
St. James-the-Less	1	738	714	247	1699
St. Jude's	2	58	108	239	405
St. Peter's	2	113	27	79	219
St. Simon Zelotes'	2	65	111	223	399
St. Andrew's	3	105	254	170	529
St. Matthew's	3	100	214	368	682
St. Barnabas'	4	44	99	136	279
St. Bartholomew's	4	37	85	88	210
St. James-the-Great	4	46	150	191	387
St. John the Evangelist	4	58	124	130	312
St. Thomas'	4	36	89	225	350

Conclusions

Taken together, these twenty parishes provide the following average attendance for each category of churchmanship:

	Church-manship	Men	Women	Child-ren	Total
(4 examples)	1	234	255	150	638
(5 examples)	2	76	110	162	348
(3 examples)	3	78	168	193	438

Church-manship	Men	Women	Child-ren	Total
(7 examples)	4	50	110	150	311
(1 example)	5	204	214	674	1092

This is somewhat deceptive, however, since the high attendance at St. James-the-Less, Bethnal Green, greatly inflates the first category, and St. Peter's, London Docks, is the only example of the fifth. Removing these two parishes from consideration, then, the following everages are produced:

Church-manship	Men	Women	Child-ren	Total
(3 examples)	1	66	101	117	284
(5 examples)	2	76	110	162	348
(3 examples)	3	78	168	193	438
(7 examples)	4	50	110	150	311

While for the reasons outlined above (especially the small nature of the sample) these figures do not furnish a basis for drawing firm conclusions, they are at least suggestive. They provide no evidence for the usual thesis that anglo-catholic parishes were more successful in attracting the poor. Nor, on the contrary, do they suggest that the evangelical parishes were any better attended. What they do indicate is that, except for the few parishes headed by charismatic pastors, the church going habits of people in the East End differed very little from those of other Englishmen. Children predominated, and the number of men was significantly less than the number of women. People were drawn, on the whole, to churches where the liturgy was not extreme in either direction. The best attended group of parishes was that in which candles were lighted during the weekly celebration of the communion, hardly a high level of churchmanship for the turn of the century. A computer based study of church attendance and churchmanship in all the London parishes of the time might well provide some interesting, and much more definite, correlations. But an impressionistic survey of Mudie-Smith and the *T.C.G.* suggests that such a study would be unlikely to disprove the conclusions drawn from the twenty parishes in St. George's-in-the-East and Bethnal Green.

NOTES

Chapter I

1. Vera Leff and G. H. Blunden, *The Story of Tower Hamlets* (London: Research Writers, 1967), 11.

2. Gareth Stedman Jones, *Outcast London: A Study in the Relationship Between Classes in Victorian Society* (Oxford: Clarendon Press, 1971), 179.

3. Robert Sinclair, *East London: The East and North-East Boroughs of London and Greater London*, Vol. XXX of the County Book Series (London: Robert Hale, 1950), 223.

4. Peter Wyld, *Stepney Story: A Thousand Years of St. Dunstan's* (London: Saint Catherine Press, 1952), 51.

5. Entry for 15 Jan. 1777; Nehemiah Curnock, ed.. *The Journal of the Rev. John Wesley, A.M.* (8 vols.; London: Epworth, 1938), VI, 136.

6. Sinclair, 237-38.

7. The outstanding economic history of Victorian London is that by G. S. Jones. Unfortunately, his Marxist bias leads him to reduce the entire "social problem" of the area to economics. His argument in Part III is, therefore, unconvincing, but no other work on East London's nineteenth century economy approaches his for thoroughness and careful scholarship.

8. H. J. Dyos, "The Slums of Victorian London," *Victorian Studies,* XI (1967), 9.

9. Perhaps, however, the effort was not as successful as the companies believed. One retired docker told me that he and his colleagues at the London Docks in Wapping (where wine, tobacco, and other valuable cargoes were required by law to be unloaded) regularly broke into the stores of liquor. In 1958 or 1959 they actually tapped a cask of ancient port that the Portuguese government had sent as a gift to Prince Philip. Interview with Harry Carleton at the public house of the White Swan, Wapping, in Dec. 1972.

10. Jones, 180.

11. Dyos, 36-37.

12. Dyos, 33.

13. Jones, 232.

14. Jones, 29.

15. Jones, 23-24, 100-01.

16. Dyos, 6.

17. John Hollingshead, *Ragged London in 1861* (London, 1861), 59-60.

18. Harry Jones, *East and West London: Being Notes of Common Life and Pastoral Work in St. James, Westminster, and in St. George's-in-the-East* (London, 1875), 2-3.

19. Walter Besant, *East London* (London, 1901), 127.

20. Besant, 8-9, 16, 38, 46.

21. Jones, 11.

22. Jones, 14.

23. Asa Briggs, *Victorian Cities* (Harmondsworth: Penguin, 1968 [1963]), 314. The term "East End" has now lost most of the opprobrium it once connoted and has even become a source of some marginal pride. I shall, therefore, use the term despite Sinclair's repeated dissuasives.

24. Sinclair, 271.

25. Charles Booth et al, *Life and Labour of the People in London,* 3rd series (7 vols.; London, 1902-03), II, 11.

26. C. F. G. Masterman, *The Condition of England* (London, 1909), 72.

27. *Life and Labour of the People in London,* 1st series (4 vols.; London, 1889-92), I, 37.

28. W. H. Hutton, ed., *Robert Gregory, 1819-1911: Being the Autobiography of Robert Gregory, D.D., Dean of St. Paul's* (London, 1912), 160.

29. Owen Chadwick, *The Victorian Church* (2 vols.; New York: Oxford University Press, 1966-1970), I, 331.

30. William Crouch, *Bryan King and the Riots at St. George's-in-the-East* (London, 1904), 21.

31. Desmond Bowen, *The Idea of the Victorian Church: A Study of the Church of England, 1833-1889* (Montreal: McGill University Press, 1968), 286.

32. Brian Heeney, "The Theory of Pastoral Ministry in the Mid-Victorian Church of England," *Historical Magazine of the Protestant Episcopal Church,* XLIII (1974), 216-17.

33. Besant, 327.

34. Chadwick, I, 331.

35. Frederick Maurice, *The Life of Frederick Denison Maurice: Chiefly Told in his own Letters* (2 vols.; London, 1884), II, 85-86.

36. John F. Porter and William J. Wolf, eds., *Toward the Recovery of Unity* (New York: Seabury, 1964), 3.

37. Chadwick has described (I, 363-69) Mann's procedure. The results were published in *Parliamentary Papers,* 1852-53, Vol. LXXXIX, "Religious Worship (England and Wales)." K. S. Inglis has written a very useful article summarizing the survey: "Patterns of Religious Worship in 1851," *Journal of Ecclesiastical History, XI* (1960), 74-86.

38. *P.P..* clvii, cxlix.

39. A very helpful book in establishing the chronology is Gordon Barnes, *Stepney Churches* (London: Faith Press, 1967).

40. Of these 49 churches, only 19 remain today. Bishop Willington-Ingram closed six as redundant between 1911 and 1930. The rest were destroyed, or sufficiently weakened so that they were never restored, during the Battle of Britain. The East end suffered far more from German bombing than any comparable area of England.

Chapter II

1. Henry Parry Liddon, *Life of Edward Bouverie Pusey* (4 vols.; London, 1893-97), III, 32. Pusey's bishop, Samuel Wilberforce, agreed. In a letter to W. J. Butler of Wantage he wrote: "I quite long to go and cast myself into that [St. George's] mission." Reginald Wilberforce, *Life of the Rt. Rev. Samuel Wilberforce* (3 vols.; London, 1880-83), II, 341.

2. Chadwick, II, 312.

3. A Tindal Hart, *The Curate's Lot: The Story of the Unbeneficed English Clergy* (London: John Baker, 1970), 190.

4. Since most of the anglo-catholics were concentrated in southern England, however, a comparison between East End parishes and those in the rest of the south would reveal a less significant difference between the proportions that were anglo-catholic. The information can be drawn from a remarkably helpful publication by the English Church Union, the *Tourist's Church Guide* (25th ed.; London, 1901). The *T.C.G.* was published bi-annually until the E.C.U. discovered that it was more useful to "no-popery" agitators than to travelling high churchmen. Owen Chadwick has summarized its statistics for four years (II, 319); his summary must be treated with caution, however, for he has failed to compare its entries with a complete list of English parishes, and thus his figures do not provide (as he suggests they do) the actual proportion of parishes with various catholic usages. The *T.C.G.* claimed to include every English parish with at least one Sunday communion, together with such details of its churchmanship as the use of the eastward position, mixed chalice, incense, vestments, altar candles, and numbers of communion services. Comparing the *T.C.G.* entries with the list of all East End parishes in *Crockford's Clerical Directory* (35th ed.; London, 1903), I have found that somewhat more than one-third of those parishes used vestments; three of the six churches in St. George's-in-the-East, five of the fourteen churches in Bethnal Green, and two of the six churches in Shoreditch. Neither of the two churches in Mile End New Town used vestments, and there are too many discrepancies between the *T.C.G.* and *Crockford's* to elicit any accurate figures for Whitechapel (though that was not a district notable for anglo-catholics). Only

four East End churches had advanced beyond vestments to the use of incense, as well: St. Peter's, London Docks; St. Michael's, Shoreditch; Holy Trinity, Shoreditch; and St. Augustine's, Whitechapel.

5. Richard Mudie-Smith, ed., *The Religious Life of London* (London, 1904), 37. See my appendix on "Churchmanship and Church Attendance."

6. The principal sources for Lowder's life and the history of the St. George's Mission are: [Maria Trench], *Charles Lowder: A Biography* (6th ed.; London, 1882); Lowder's two books, *Ten Years in S. George's Mission* (London, 1867) and *Twenty-One Years in S. George's Mission* (London, 1877); the extensive records retained at St. Peter's, London Docks; Lida E. Ellsworth, "Charles Lowder and the Ritualist Movement" (Ph.D. thesis, Cambridge University, 1974); and L. E. Ellsworth, *Charles Lowder and the Ritualist Movement* (London: Darton, Longman and Todd, 1982). There is also a surprisingly good, hagiographical novel about Lowder: Ann Stafford, *Light Me a Candle* (London: Hodder and Stoughton, 1949).

7. *Twenty-One Years,* 14.

8. Trench, 29.

9. Such Continental visits by anglo-catholics seem to have been common at least later in the century, though for obvious reasons (the possible incitement of "no-popery" fears) they were not often discussed. It would be difficult to overstress the separation between Anglican and Roman Catholic in Victorian England. Newman's account of that separation in the *Apologia* is well known. But what many do not realize is that the separation has only begun to break down within the last twenty-five years. The late Canon Cheslyn Jones, former Principal of Chichester Theological College, told me that for nearly ten years he had encountered almost daily the Roman Catholic priest in Chichester. Nothing more than the severest formalities had passed between them until the 1966 meeting of Arthur Michael Ramsey, Archbishop of Canterbury, and Pope Paul VI. On that very day, the Roman Catholic priest addressed Canon Jones by name and asked him home for a drink, saying, "Your boss has met my boss. It's time we got together." This is remarkable, for Canon Jones was as anglo-catholic who had been close to many Continental Roman Catholics since the end of the Second World War. But until that 1966 meeting, he had never met an English Roman Catholic priest in any but the most formal setting.

10. *Twenty-One Years,* 15-16.

11. My own periphrastic translation from Abelly's text as quoted in the Ellsworth thesis, 71-72.

12. Ellsworth thesis, 72, quoting from the 1856 records of the S.S.C.

13. Trench, 48.

14. *Twenty-One Years,* 83.

15. "Annual Report for 1862," 10.

16. "Annual Report for 1863," 2.

17. "Annual Report for 1858," 3.

18. Trench, 148.

19. Oral tradition in the parish holds that the choice of a title was made by the bishop over Lowder's objections. At the time of the Trench biography, the church was generally known as St. Peter's-in-the-East. Only after Lowder's death did it receive the informal designation it still carries, St. Peter's, London Docks.

20. Technically, Lowder remained "Perpetual Curate" for several years, until the Rector of St. George's finally relinquished his purely titular precedence over the new parish.

21. "Annual Report for 1857," 6.

22. Trench, 232.

23. Letter in lieu of the 1868 annual report, 2. But Lowder's parochial resolve was short-lived; the "Annual Report of the S. George's Mission" resumed in 1869 and continued until well after Lowder's death.

24. Ellsworth thesis, 179, quoting from the 1868 records of the S.S.C.

25. "Annual Report for 1878," 4.

26. "Annual Report for 1858," 8.

27. Ellsworth thesis, 109.

28. "Annual Report for 1863," 12.

29. "Annual Report for 1865," 9. The anglo-catholic slum clergy universally rejected the common argument that relief was corrupting to the recipient, probably because the notion of charity had such a firm hold in the catholic tradition. In the "Annual Report for 1884" Wainright wrote (6) "Then comes relief--a bad thing say many--it pauperizes people and makes them lazy. It destroys the relation, so they will have it, between the Priest and his people and turns him into a Relieving Officer. And what else, I should ask, is he than a Relieving Officer ?" Oral tradition in the parish recounts frequent instances of Wainright's giving away not only his money but his clothes, blankets, and linens, as well. It is clear that only his more sensible curates stood between Wainright and utter destitution.

30. *Twenty-One Years*, 202.

31. *Twenty-One Years*, 210.

32. *Twenty-One Years*, 210.

33. Trench, 223.

34. "Annual Report for 1866," 6.

35. *Twenty-One Years*, 213.

36. Trench, 227.

37. Trench, 227.

38. Trench, 249.

39. *Twenty-One Years*, 104.

40. "Annual Report for 1861," 6.

41. "Annual Report for 1864," 4.

42. C. F. Lowder, "Five Years in S. George's Mission" (London, 1861), 48.

43. *Twenty-One Years,* 148.

44. "Annual Report for 1862," 12.

45. "Annual Report for 1871," 6.

46. *Twenty-One Years,* 56-58.

47. "Annual Report for 1874," 6-7.

48. *Twenty-One Years,* 61.

49. Linklater's own account of his mission is found in Trench, 250-63, and in *Twenty-One Years,* 169-91.

50. *Twenty-One Years,* 167.

51. *Twenty-One Years,* 50, 55, 100.

52. "Annual Report for 1859," 7.

53. Trench, 289-91.

54. *Church Times,* 24 Sept. 1880.

55. Lucy Menzies, *Father Wainright: A Record* (London: Longmans, Green, 1947), 21.

56. *Life and Labour,* 3rd series, II, 35-36.

Chapter III

1. [Henrietta Rowland Barnett], *Canon Barnett: His Life, Work and Friends* (2 vols.; London, 1918), I, 68. Much of the biography is drawn from Barnett's papers and letters, most of which are now deposited at the Greater London Record Office.

2. "Recalling 2 true founders of the Welfare State," in *Church Times* (15 Dec. 1972), 11.

3. C. K. Francis Brown, *A History of the English Clergy, 1800-1900* (London: Faith Press, 1953), 231. Brown suggests that Clémenceau was "the last person to be sentimental about an English clergyman."

4. *Canon Barnett,* II, 97-98.

5. Samuel A. Barnett, *The Service of God: Sermons, Essays, and Addresses* (London, 1897), 166.

6. *Canon Barnett,* I, 13.

7. *Canon Barnett,* I, 12.

8. *Canon Barnett,* I, 22-23.

9. Beatrice Webb, *My Apprenticeship* (Harmondsworth: Penguin, 1971 [1926]), 219.

10. *Canon Barnett,* I, 284.

11. *The Toynbee Record,* XXV (July-Sept. 1913), 145.

12. Webb, 206.

13. *Canon Barnett*, I, 29.

14. *Canon Barnett*, I, 83.

15. "St. Jude's Whitechapel: 17th Pastoral Address and Report of the Parish Work" (London, 1890), 29. A surviving copy of this report is now in the British Museum.

16. S. A. Barnett, "Sermon Preached before the University of Oxford, 15 June 1884," 3.

17. *Canon Barnett*, II, 231, 263.

18. "17th Pastoral Address," 20.

19. *Canon Barnett*, I, 82.

20. *Canon Barnett*, I, 105, 107.

21. *Canon Barnett*, I, 182. It is therefore amusing to find Barnett complaining later (*Service of God*, 299) that "The time of the clergy is inordinately taken up in starting clubs and attending committees."

22. *Canon Barnett*, I, 284.

23. *Canon Barnett*, I. 132.

24. *Canon Barnett*, II, 311.

25. *Canon Barnett*, I, 89-90.

26. *Canon Barnett*, I, 79.

27. *Canon Barnett*, I, 77.

28. *Canon Barnett*, I, 281.

29. *Canon Barnett*, I, 280.

30. *Service of God*, 301. S. A. and H. O. Barnett, *Practicable Socialism: Essays on Social Reform*, 2nd ed. (London, 1894), 197.

31. *St. Jude's* (The Parish Magazine of St. Jude's Whitechapel), I (Dec. 1889), 106; I (Jan. 1889), 5. This rather substantial (8-12 page) monthly magazine, published from 1889 to 1893 and now preserved in the British Museum, provides the most important evidence for the Barnetts' last years in the parish.

32. *Canon Barnett*, I, 200.

33. *Canon Barnett*, I, 326-31.

34. "17th Pastoral Address," 38.

35. *Canon Barnett*, II, 169; I, 95.

36. *Canon Barnett*, I, 219.

37. *Canon Barnett*, II, 157.

38. *Canon Barnett*, I, 156.

39. *Canon Barnett*, I, 161.

40. *Canon Barnett*, I, 152.

41. *Canon Barnett*, I, 160. Henrietta Barnett had the irritating habit of referring to these gatherings as *conversaziones*.

42. *Canon Barnett*, I, 158, 162.

43. *Canon Barnett*, I, 186.

44. *Canon Barnett*, II, 274.

45. *Canon Barnett*, I, 76.

46. *Canon Barnett*, II, 134.

47. *Canon Barnett*, II, 135.

48. *St. Jude's*, I (Jan. 1889), 3.

49. *Service of God*, 299.

50. *St. Jude's* , III (Feb. 1891), 9.

51. H. O. Barnett, ed. *Vision and Service: Being Sermons, Papers, Letters, and Aphorisms by Canon Barnett* (London, n.d. [1917]), 13.

52. *Canon Barnett*, I, 193; II, 9.

53. *Canon Barnett*, II, 66.

54. Peter d'A Jones, *The Christian Socialist Revival 1877-1914: Religion, Class, and Social Conscience in Late-Victorian England* (Princeton: Princeton University Press, 1968), 181-83.

55. *St. Jude's*, I (Oct. 1889), 95.

56. *Canon Barnett*, II, 67.

57. *St. Jude's*, V (Sept. 1893), 82.

58. In *St. Jude's*, IV (July 1892), Barnett discussed the rival candidates with a perfect neutrality.

59. *Vision and Service*, 68.

60. Samuel A. Barnett, *Religion and Politics: Lectures Given in Westminster Abbey* (London, 1911), 132.

61. *Religion and Politics*, 141.

62. *Service of God*, 148-50.

63. *Service of God*, 3.

64. *Canon Barnett*, II, 39.

65. Chadwick, II, 277; Barnett, *Practicable Socialism*, 241-50.

66. *Service of God*, 11-12.

67. *St. Jude's*, I (April, 1889), 88.

68. *St. Jude's*, IV (April 1892), 27.

59. *Service of God*, 298.

Chapter IV

1. G. R. Balleine, *A History of the Evangelical Party in the Church of England* (London, 1909), 237.

2. Islington Church Extension Society, *Report of Proceedings* (London, 1857), 23. I am indebted to K. S. Inglis, *Churches and theWorking Classes in Victorian England* (London: Routledge and Kegan Paul, 1963), 371, for this citation.

3. Balleine, 238. *Parliamentary Papers*, Vol. IX, 1857-58, "The Deficiency of Means of Spiritual Instruction and Places of Divine Worship in the Me-

tropolis," 124.

    4. Service Book of St. Mary's, Whitechapel, 1847-70, Greater London
Record Office.

    5. It is clear that Watts-Ditchfield assumed, rather than inherited, his
hyphenated name.

    6. Ellis N. Gowing, *John Edwin Watts-Ditchfield: First Bishop of
Chelmsford* (London: Hodder and Stoughton, n.d. [1927]).

    7. Interviews with Mrs. Dorothy M. Watts-Ditchfield Gowing at
Southend-on-Sea, Dec. 1972, and with the Rev. John E. Gowing at London, Jan.
1973. The best evidence for Watts-Ditchfield's life would be the diary he kept
faithfully from his childhood until his death in 1923. Unfortunately for historians, his daughter gave more than fifty volumes of this diary to the first wartime
scrap-paper drive in 1939.

    8. Gowing, 20-21.

    9. Gowing, 13-14. J. E. Watts-Ditchfield, *Fishers of Men or How to
Win the Men* (London, n.d. [1899]), 117.

    10. Gowing, 14.

    11. Gowing, 26.

    12. Gowing, 31.

    13. This magazine is now in the possession of the present vicar. Many
other records were lost when the west end of the church was fire-bombed during
the Second World War.

    14. Interview with the Rev. Ted Roberts, Vicar of St. James-the-Less,
Bethnal Green, Oct. 1972.

    15. George A. Leask, "The Rev. J. E. Watts-Ditchfield at Bethnal
Green," *Sunday at Home* (1904), 169.

    16. Gowing, 59.

    17. *Fishers of Men*, 94ff.

    18. Gowing, 71, and the 1912 parish magazine.

    19. Since he normally preached extemporaneously within his own par-
ish, most of his seventeen surviving sermons were those delivered at St. Paul's
Cathedral, at Westminster Abbey, or before the University of Cambridge. Sixteen
are collected in J. E. Watts-Ditchfield, *Here and Hereafter* (London, 1911). The
other is a remarkably balanced view of Jewish immigration to the East End:
"The Church and the Alien and the Anarchist," in Percy Dearmer, ed., *Sermons
on Social Subjects* (London, 1911), 23-36.

    20. *Here and Hereafter*, 85-86, 126, 82.

    21. *Here and Hereafter*, 133, 135, 136.

    22. Dearmer, 33.

    23. *Here and Hereafter*, 130.

    24. Gowing, 260.

    25. *Here and Hereafter*, 96, 124. J. E. Watts-Ditchfield, *The Church in*

Action: Lectures delivered in the Divinity School of the University of Cambridge in 1913 (London, 1913), 125.

    26. *Fishers of Men*, 86.

    27. Gowing, 88.

    28. A recollection of Ellis N. Gowing, as told to his son, John E. Gowing.

    29. Gowing, 84.

    30. *Fishers of Men*, 22-23.

    31. The ordinations occurred on 17 Dec. 1972, accompanied by recorded American gospel music. See Ted Roberts, *Partners and Ministers* (London: Falcon, 1972). Roberts, who conceived the scheme in ignorance of Watts-Ditchfield's writings on the subject, had good reason for understanding the workingman's alienation from the church; his own father was an automobile mechanic just beyond the borders of his parish.

    32. Raymond Blathwayt, "The Rev. J. E. Watts-Ditchfield," *The Treasury*, III (April 1904), 2.

    33. *Fishers of Men*, 128.

    34. *Here and Hereafter*, 135.

    35. Gowing, 35.

    36. Blathwayt, 3.

    37. Gowing, 249.

    38. J. E. Watts-Ditchfield, *The Church in Action* (London, 1913), 21-22. In the same lectures he was punctilious in his directions for celebrating the communion; e.g., 52: "Things which may seem minute and even trivial must be watched." Cf. *Here and Hereafter*, 61: "Therefore, the Holy Communion must ever be treasured by those who love their Lord."

    39. *Here and Hereafter*, 202-31.

    40. *The Guardian*, 2 Aug. 1912.

    41. J. E. Watts-Ditchfield and C. Gore, *Reservation* (London, 1917).

    42. *The Guardian*, 22 Oct. 1920; *Church Times*, 15 Oct. 1920.

    43. *Times*, 28 May 1923.

    44. Mudie-Smith, 49-61. The survey lists 1699 who attended St. James-the Less and another 647 who attended one of its missions. In fact, only one church in the East End--the Roman Catholic church on Commercial Road--had a larger congregation.

    45. Ted Roberts, "Evangelism in Industrial Parishes" (unpublished essay, 1965).

    46. Blathwayt, 2-3.

    47. Leask, 170.

    48. *Fishers of Men*, 117.

    49. Gowing, 49.

    50. Gowing, 148.

51. Roberts, "Evangelism in Industrial Parishes."

52. Charles Booth visited the Men's Service twice in its early days. Of the first occasion he wrote: "The body of the church was full of men, not less than 500, I thought. Looking at them from my seat at the back I took them to be mostly above working-class level, but studying them later as they left the building one could see that a large proportion were either artisans or the sons of working men employed as clerks." Later Booth wrote: "On the occasion of the second visit, made a year later, the men only loosely filled the body of the church, which might mean 300. All ages were represented, inclining to young, and there were some possibly of middle class; but the general bulk were lower middle and upper working class, with no very wide divergence amongst them." *Life and Labour*, 3rd series, I, 240-41.

53. Inglis, 304. The worst of Victorian evangelicalism has often been satirized, but it does not require the parodist's pen. C. Maurice Davies, writing about "Fashionable Evangelicalism" or "the Lavender Kid Glove School of Theology" in *Orthodox London: Or, Phases of Religious Life in the Church of England* (London, 1876), 91, recorded an engraved invitation that he had actually seen:

Mr._____

and Miss_____ propose (D.V.) to hold a Bible Reading

on _____ Evening, _____, at 7 1/2

o'Clock, when the Company of Friends is requested.

Subject, Rev.ii

Reading from 7 3/4 to 9 1/2

Morning Dress

54. Alexander Zabriskie, ed., *Anglican Evangelicalism* (Philadelphia: The Church Historical Society, 1943), 19-21. Zabriskie writes that in the early nineteenth century "...the Evangelicals had not been identified with the low church group; the latitudinarians had occupied that position, against whom the Evangelicals had protested that they were Socinians."

Chapter V

1. Anon., "Home Mission-Work in Large Towns," *Church Quarterly Review*, XXII (1886), 287.

2. James G. Adderley, *Looking Upward: Papers Introductory to the Study of Social Questions from a Religious Point of View* (London, 1896), 15.

3. *Life and Labour*, 3rd series, I, 32-33; cf. 38-40. The activities included two temperance societies, a men's club, seven boys' clubs, four girls' clubs, five children's guilds, a benefit society, a penny bank, a parish library, and various parish schools, Sunday schools, and bible classes.

4. *East London*, 331. Besant added, however: "Never before, alas! has the Church possessed so few scholars or so few preachers. Learning, save for a scholar here and there, has deserted the Church of England."

5. "A Riverside Parish," in Robert A. Woods, ed., *The Poor in Great Cities: Their Problems and What is Being Done to Solve Them* (London, 1896), 240-74.

6. "A Riverside Parish," 257, 262, 264.

7. Besant, 327-28.

8. Inglis, 34-35.

9. *Life and Labour*, 3rd series, I, 34-35.

10. *East and West London*, 47, 49, 59, 63.

11. *Life and Labour*, 3rd series, I, 38.

12. Besant, 329.

13. Mudie-Smith, 24-25.

14. Inglis has calculated ("Patterns of Religious Worship," 85) that 29.7% of East Enders attended worship in 1851. Working from Mudie-Smith's 1902-03 results (22-24), the corresponding figure is 19.5%. This decline in the number of worshippers is corroborated by the results of W. R. Nicholl's religious census of 24 Oct. 1886, undertaken for the *British Weekly*. The results for the East End are presented by Booth in *Life and Labour*, 1st series, I, Table XIX. Nicholl concluded that of the approximately one half million East End residents who could have attended church on that particular Sunday, only 23.6% did so. His actual figures--i.e., the percentage of the entire population (including infants, the sick, and those who worked on Sunday) who attended--are even lower. Arranged by districts, they are: Shoreditch--11%; Bethnal Green--13%; Whitechapel--11%; St. George's-in-the-East--11%; Stepney--12%; Mile End Old Town--15%; Poplar--17%; Hackney--40%; total for the East End--17%.

15. Sinclair, 75.

16. Foreword to Roberts, *Partners and Ministers*, 7. Sinclair, 78.

17. Mudie-Smith, 7-13, 25.

18. E. R. Wickham, *Church and People in an Industrial City* (London: Lutterworth, 1957), 176. I have been unable to locate the passage in Booth.

19. Arthur F. Winnington-Ingram, *Work in Great Cities: Six Lectures on Pastoral Theology* (London, 1896), 22.

20. "Home Mission-Work in Large Towns," 297.

21. Mudie-Smith, 196.

22. "On Being a Mid-Victorian Clergyman," 209, 214, 222, 224.

23. G. S. Jones makes roughly this same argument with regard to the C.O.S. in *Outcast London*, part III.

SELECTED BIBLIOGRAPHY

A. Archive Collections

Greater London Record Office: Records of St. Jude's, Whitechapel.
Greater London Record Office: Records of St. Mary Matfelon, Whitechapel.
Greater London Record Office: Records of Toynbee Hall.
St. James-the-Less, Bethnal Green: Records of the parish.
St. Peter's, London Docks: Records of the parish.

B. Periodicals, Annual Reports, and Year Books

Annual Reports of St. George's Mission, 1857-1914.
The Church Times, 1869-1914.
Crockford's Clerical Directory, 1870-1910.
The Guardian, 1850-1914.
The Record, 1837-1914.
St. James-the-Less Monthly Magazine, Jan. 1912.
St. Jude's (The Parish Magazine of St. Jude's, Whitechapel), vols. I-V
    (1889-93).
St. Peter's [London Docks] Parish Magazine, Dec. 1889.

C. Contemporary Works

Adderley, James G. *Looking Upward: Papers Introductory to the Study
    of Social Questions from a Religious Point of View.* London,
    1896.
_____. *The Parson in Socialism.* London, 1910.
_____. *In Slums and Society.* London, 1916.
_____. *Stephen Remarx.* London, 1893.

Baring-Gould, Sabine. *The Church Revival.* London, 1914.

Barnett, Henrietta O., ed. *Vision and Service: Being Sermons, Papers, Letters, and Aphorisms by Canon Barnett.* London, n.d. [1917].

_____. ed. *Worship and Work: Thoughts from the Unpublished Writings of the Late Canon S. A. Barnett.* Letchworth, 1914.

Barnett, Samuel A. *The Ideal City.* Bristol, 1894.

_____. *Religion and Politics: Lectures Given in Westminster Abbey.* London, 1911.

_____. *Religion and Progress.* London, 1907.

_____. "St. Jude's, Whitechapel: 17th Pastoral Address and Report of the Parish Work." London, 1890.

_____. "Settlements of University Men in Great Towns." (A paper delivered at Oxford University, 17 Nov. 1883.) Oxford, 1884.

_____. "Sermon Preached before the University of Oxford, 15 June 1884." Oxford, 1884.

_____. *The Service of God: Sermons, Essays, and Addresses.* London, 1897.

_____. and Henrietta O. Barnett. *Practicable Socialism.* 2nd ed. London, 1894.

_____. *Towards Social Reform.* London, 1909.

Besant, Walter. *All Sorts and Conditions of Men.* London, 1883.

_____. *East London.* London, 1901.

_____. "A Riverside Parish." *The Poor in Great Cities: Their Problems and What Is Being Done to Solve Them.* Edited by Robert A. Woods. London, 1896.

Blathwayt, Raymond. "The Rev. J. E. Watts-Ditchfield." *The Treasury,* III (April 1904), 1-5.

Booth, Charles, et al. *Life and Labour of the People in London.* First Series. 4 vols. London, 1889-92.

_____. *Life and Labour of the People in London.* Third Series. 7 vols. London, 1902-03.

Bosanquet, Bernard, ed. *Aspects of the Social Problem.* London, 1895.

Champneys, W. Weldon. *The Spirit and the Word: Facts Gathered from a Thirty Years' Ministry.* London, 1862.

Davies, C. Maurice. *Orthodox London: Or, Phases of Religious Life in the Church of England.* London, 1876.

Dearmer, Percy. *Sermons on Social Subjects.* London, 1911.

Dolling, Robert F. *Ten Years in a Portsmouth Slum.* London, 1897.

Fried, Albert, and Richard M. Elman, eds. *Charles Booth's London.* Harmondsworth: Penguin, 1971 [1969].

Gell, Philip L. "The Municipal Responsibilities of the 'Well-to-Do." London, n.d.

Greenwood, James. *The Seven Curses of London*. London, 1869.

Hadden, R. H. *An East-End Chronicle: St. George's-in-the-East Parish and Parish Church*. London, 1880.

Haw, G., ed. *Christianity and the Working Classes*. London, 1896.

Headlam, Stewart D. *The Meaning of the Mass*. London, 1908.

_____. *The Socialist Church*. London, 1907.

Hocking, W. J., ed. *The Church and New Century Problems*. London, 1901.

Holland, Henry Scott. *The Labour Movement*. London, 1897.

Hollingshead, John. *Ragged London in 1861*. London, 1861.

"Home Mission-Work in Large Towns." *Church Quarterly Review*, XXII (1886), 287-310.

Islington Church Extension Society. *Report of Proceedings*. London, 1857.

Jay, A. Osborne. *Life in Darkest London: A Hint to General Booth*. London, 1891.

_____. *A Story of Shoreditch: Being a Sequel to "Life in Darkest London"*. London, 1896.

Jones, Harry. *East and West London: Being Notes of Common Life and Pastoral Work in St. James, Westminster, and in St. George's-in-the-East*. London, 1875.

_____. *Priest and Parish*. London, 1866.

King, Bryan. "Sacrilege and its Encouragement." London, 1860.

Lambert, H. Brooke. "East London Pauperism: A sermon to the University of Oxford." Oxford, 1868.

_____. *Pauperism: Seven Sermons Preached at St. Mark's, Whitechapel*. London, 1871.

"A Layman." "The Riots at St. George's East: A Letter to the Lord Bishop of London." London, 1860.

Leask, George A. "The Rev. J. E. Watts-Ditchfield at Bethnal Green." *Sunday at Home*, Dec. 1904, 169-73.

Leighton, Sir Baldwyn, ed. *Letters and Other Writings of the Late Edward Denison, M.P., for Newark*. London, 1875.

Liddon, Henry Parry. "The Aims and Principles of Church Missions." *Sermons Preached on Special Occasions, 1860-1889*. London, 1889.

Lowder, Charles F. "Five Years at S. George's Mission." London, 1861.

_____.   "Sacramental Confession Examined by Pastoral Experi-
ence." London, 1874.

_____.   "S. Katharine's Hospital: Its History and Revenues, and
their Application to Missionary Purposes in the East of London." London, 1867.

_____. *Ten Years in Saint George's Mission.* London,1867.

_____. *Twenty-One Years in S. George's Mission.* London,1877.

Mackeson, Charles. *A Guide to the Churches of London.* London, 1866.

_____.   *A Guide to the Churches of London and its Suburbs.* Lon-
don, 1883.

Masterman, C. F. G. *The Condition of England.* London, 1909.

Mayhew, Henry, *London Characters.* London, 1870.

_____.   *London Labour and the London Poor.* 4 vols. London,
1861.

Morrison, Arthur. *A Child of the Jago.* Edited by P. J. Keating. London:
MacGibbon and Kee, 1969 [1894].

_____. *Tales of Mean Streets.* London, 1892.

Mudie-Smith, Richard, ed. *The Religious Life of London.* (The *Daily
News* census of 1902-03.) London, 1904.

Parliamentary Papers, 1857-58, Vol. IX. "The Deficiency of Means of
Spiritual Instruction and Places of Worship in the Metropolis."

Parliamentary Papers. 1852-53, Vol. LXXXIX. "Religious Worship (England and
Wales)."

[Preston, William.] "The Bitter Cry of Outcast London: An Enquiry
into the Condition of the Abject Poor." Also attributed to Andrew
Mearns. London, 1883.

Secretary of the English Church Union, ed. *Tourist's Church Guide.* 19th
ed. London, 1890.

_____. *Tourist's Church Guide.* 25th ed. London, 1901.

Shipley, Orby, ed. *The Church and the World: Essays on the Questions
of the Day in 1866.* 3rd ed. London, 1867.

_____.   *The Church and the World: Essays on the Questions of
the Day in 1867.* London, 1867.

Shuttleworth, H. C. *The Christian Church and the Problem of Poverty.*
London, 1894.

Universities' Settlement Association. "Work for University Men in East
London." London, 1884.

Walker, Henry. *East London: Sketches of Christian Work and Workers.* London, 1896.

Watts-Ditchfield, John Edwin. "The Church and the Alien and the Anarchist." *Sermons on Social Subjects.* Edited by Percy Dearmer. London, 1911.

_____. *The Church in Action.* London, 1913.

_____. *Fishers of Men, or How to Win the Men.* London, 1899.

_____. *Here and Hereafter.* London, 1911.

_____. Letter to *The Times.* 28 May 1923.

_____. and Charles Gore. *Reservation.* London, 1917.

Webb, Beatrice. *My Apprenticeship.* Harmondsworth: Penguin, 1971 [1926].

_____. *Our Partnership.* London: Allen and Unwin, 1948.

Winnington-Ingram, Arthur F. *Work in Great Cities: Six Lectures on Pastoral Theology.* London, 1896.

D. Biographies

Aitken, W. Francis. *Canon Barnett, Warden of Toynbee Hall: His Mission and its Relation to Social Movements.* London, 1902.

[Barnett, Henrietta O.] *Canon Barnett: His Life, Work, and Friends.* 2 vols. London, 1918.

Battiscombe, Georgina. *John Keble: A Study in Limitations.* London: Constable, 1963.

Bayne, G. *Brooke Lambert: Sermons and Lectures and a Memoir.* London, 1902.

Bennett, F. *The Story of W. J. E. Bennett.* London, 1909.

Bettany, F. G. *Stewart Headlam: A Biography.* London: John Murray, 1926.

Blomfield, Alfred. *A Memoir of Charles James Blomfield, D.D., with Selections from his Correspondence.* 2 vols. London, 1863.

Brill, Kenneth, ed. *John Groser: East London Priest.* London: Mowbrays, 1971.

Bullock, Charles. *The Crown of the Road: Leaves from Consecrated Lives.* London, 1884.

[Butler, A. J.] *Life and Letters of William John Butler.* London, 1897.

Carpenter, S. C. *Winnington-Ingram: The Biography of Arthur Foley Winnington-Ingram, Bishop of London, 1901-1939.* London: Hodder and Stoughton, 1949.

Clayton, Joseph. *Father Stanton of St. Alban's, Holborn: A Memoir.* London, 1913.

London, 1913.

Crouch, William. *Bryan King and the Riots at St. George's-in-the-East.* London, 1904.

Davidson, Randall T. *Life of Archibald Campbell Tait, Archbishop of Canterbury.* 2 vols. London, 1891.

Foakes, Grace. *Between High Walls: A London Childhood.* London: Shepheard-Walwyn, 1972.

Gavin, Hector. *Sanitary Ramblings: Being Sketches and Illustrations of Bethnal Green, a Type of the Condition of the Metropolis.* London, 1848.

Gowing, Ellis N. *John Edwin Watts-Ditchfield: First Bishop of Chelmsford.* London: Hodder and Stoughton, 1926.

Head, F. W. *Six Great Anglicans: A Study of the History of the Church of England in the Nineteenth Century.* London: SCM, 1929.

How, Frederick Douglas. *Bishop Walsham How: A Memoir.* London, 1898.

Hutton, W. H., ed. *Robert Gregory, 1819-1911: Being the Autobiography of Robert Gregory, D.D., Dean of St. Paul's.* London, 1912.

Liddon, Henry Parry. *Life of Edward Bouverie Pusey.* 4 vols. London, 1893-97.

Maurice, Frederick. *The Life of Frederick Denison Maurice: Chiefly Told in his own Letters.* 2 vols. London, 1884.

Menzies, Lucy. *Father Wainright: A Record.* London: Longmans, Green, 1947.

Osborne, Charles E. *The Life of Father Dolling.* London, 1903.

Paget, Stephen. *Henry Scott Holland: Memoir and Letters.* London: John Murray, 1921.

Reckitt, Maurice B. *For Christ and the People: Studies of Four Socialist Priests and Prophets of the Church of England between 1870 and 1930.* London: S.P.C.K., 1968.

Reynolds, Michael. *Martyr of Ritualism: Father Mackonochie of St. Alban's, Holborn.* London: Faber and Faber, 1965.

Richardson, Mrs. Thomas. *Forty Year's Ministry in East London.* London, 1903.

Russell, G. W. E. *Arthur Stanton: A Memoir*. London, 1917.

Simey, T. S., and M. B. Simey. *Charles Booth, Social Scientist*. Oxford. Oxford University Press, 1960.

[Towle, Eleanor.] *Alexander Heriot Mackonochie: A Memoir*. Edited by E. F. Russell. London, 1890.
[Trench, Maria.] *Charles Lowder: A Biography*. 6th ed. London, 1882.

Washburn, Henry Bradford. *The Religious Motive in Philanthropy: Studies in Biography*. The George Dana Boardman Lectures in Christian Ethics for 1931. Philadelphia: University of Pennsylvania Press, 1931.
Wilberforce, Reginald G. *Life of the Rt. Rev. Samuel Wilberforce*. 3 vols. London, 1880-83.

E. Other Secondary Sources

Abel, Emily K. "Canon Barnett and the First Thirty Years of Toynbee Hall." Ph.D. thesis, University of London, 1969.
Allchin, A. M. *The Silent Rebellion: Anglican Religious Communities, 1845-1900*. London, SCM, 1958.
Anson, Peter F. *The Call of the Cloister: Religious Communities and Kindred Bodies in the Anglican Communion*. Revised by A. W. Campbell. London: S.P.C.K., 1964.

Balleine, G. R. *A History of the Evangelical Party in the Church of England*. London, 1909.
Barnes, Gordon. *Stepney Churches: An Historical Account*. London: Faith Press, 1967.
Best, G. F. A. "Popular Protestantism in Victorian Britain." *Ideas and Institutions of Victorian Britain: Essays in Honour of George Kitson Clark*. Edited by Robert Robson. London: G. Bell and Sons, 1967.
_____. *Temporal Pillars: Queen Anne's Bounty, The Ecclesiastical Commissioners, and the Church of England*. Cambridge: Cambridge University Press, 1964.
Binns, Leonard Elliott. *The Evangelical Movement in the English Church*. Garden City: Doubleday, Doran, 1928.
Binyon, Gilbert Clive. *The Christian Socialist Movement in England: An Introduction to the Study of its History*. London: S.P.C.K., 1931.
Bosanquet, Helen. *Social Work in London, 1869-1912: A History of the Charity Organisation Society*. London, 1914.

Bowen, Desmond. *The Idea of the Victorian Church: A Study of the Church of England, 1833-1889*. Montreal: McGill University Press, 1968.

Briggs, Asa. *Victorian Cities*. Harmondsworth: Penguin, 1968 [1963].

Brown, C. K. Francis. *A History of the English Clergy, 1800-1900*. London: Faith Press, 1953.

Carpenter, S. C. *Church and People, 1789-1889: A History of the Church of England from William Wilberforce to "Lux Mundi"*. London: S.P.C.K., 1933.

Chadwick, Owen. *The Victorian Church*. 2 vols. Oxford: Oxford University Press, 1966-70.

Chesney, K. *The Victorian Underworld*. Harmondsworth: Penguin, 1972.

Church, R. W. *The Oxford Movement, 1833-1845*. Chicago: University of Chicago Press, 1970 [1891].

Clark, G. Kitson. *Churchmen and the Condition of England, 1832-1885*. London: Methuen, 1973.

_____. *The Making of Victorian England*. London: Methuen, 1953.

Crowther, M. A. *Church Embattled: Religious Controversy in Mid-Victorian England*. Hamden, CT: Archon Books, 1970.

Darby, Madge. *The First Hundred Years at St. Peter's, London Docks*. London: privately printed, 1966.

Davies, D. Horton M. *The Ecumenical Century, 1900-1965*. Vol. V of *Worship and Theology in England*. Princeton: Princeton University Press, 1965.

_____. *From Newman to Martineau, 1850-1900*. Vol. IV of *Worship and Theology in England*. Princeton: Princeton University Press, 1962.

_____. *From Watts and Wesley to Maurice, 1690-1850*. Vol. III of *Worship and Theology in England*. Princeton: Princeton University Press, 1961.

Dimsdale, D. C. *History of an East End Parish (Christ Church, Watney Street)*. London, 1901.

Donovan, Marcus. *After the Tractarians*. London: Philip Allan, 1933.

Draper, William H. *University Extension: A Survey of Fifty Years, 1873-1923*. Cambridge: Cambridge University Press, 1923.

Dyos, H. J. "The Slums of Victorian London." *Victorian Studies*, XI (1967), 5-40.

Ellsworth, Lida Elizabeth. "Charles Lowder and the Ritualist Movement." Ph.D.
    thesis, Cambridge University, 1974.
_____. *Charles Lowder and the Ritualist Movement*. London: Darton,
    Longman and Todd, 1982.
Embry, J. *The Catholic Movement and the Society of the Holy Cross*. London:
    Faith Press, 1931.

Gilley, Sheridan Wayne. "Evangelical and Roman Catholic Missions to the Irish
    in London, 1830-1870." Ph.D. thesis, Cambridge University, 1971.

Hart, A. Tindal. *The Curate's Lot: The Story of the Unbeneficed English Clergy*.
    London: John Baker, 1970.
Heasman, Kathleen. *Evangelicals in Action: An Appraisal of their Social Work
    in the Victorian Era*. London: Geoffrey Bles, 1962.
Heeney, Brian. *A Different Kind of Gentleman: Parish Clergy as Professional
    Men in Early and Mid-Victorian England*. Hamden, CT: Archon Books,
    1976.
_____. "On Being a Mid-Victorian Clergyman," *The Journal of
    Religious History*. VII (1973), 208-24.
_____. "The Theory of Pastoral Ministry in the Mid-Victorian Church of
    England." *Historical Magazine of the Protestant Episcopal Church*, XLIII
    (1974), 215-30.
Hennessy, George. *Novum Repertorium Ecclesiasticum Parochiale Londinense:
    Or London Diocesan Clergy Succession from the Earliest Time to the
    Year 1898*. London, 1898.
Hobshawn, E. J. *Industry and Empire*. Vol. III of the *Pelican Economic History
    of Britain*. Harmondsworth: Penguin, 1969.

Inglis, K. S. *Churches and the Working Classes in Victorian England*. London:
    Routlege and Kegan Paul, 1963.
_____. "Patterns of Religious Worship in 1851." *Journal of Ecclesiastical
    History*, XI (1960), 74-86.

Jones, Gareth Stedman. *Outcast London: A Study in the Relationship between
    Classes in Victorian Society*. Oxford: Clarendon Press, 1971.
Jones, Peter d'A. *The Christian Socialist Revival, 1877-1914: Religion, Class,
    and Social Conscience in Late-Victorian England*. Princeton: Princeton
    University Press, 1968.

Leff, Vera, and G. H. Blunden. *The Story of Tower Hamlets*. London: Research
    Writers, 1967.
Lloyd, Roger. *The Church of England, 1900-1965*. London: SCM, 1966.

Mallon, J. J. "The Story of Toynbee Hall (The Universities' Settlement in East London)." London: privately printed, 1939.
_____. "Toynbee Hall, Past and Present." London, n.d.
Marsh, P. T. *The Victorian Church in Decline: Archbishop Tait and the Church of England, 1868-1882*. London: Routledge and Kegan Paul, 1969.
Martin, David. *A Sociology of English Religion*. London, SCM, 1967.
Meacham, Standish. "The Church in the Victorian City." *Victorian Studies,* XI (1967), 359-78.

Owen, D. *English Philanthropy, 1660-1960*. Cambridge: Harvard University Press, 1964.

Peck, William George. *The Social Implications of the Oxford Movement*. New York: Charles Scribner's Sons, 1933.
Pimlott, J. A. R. *Toynbee Hall: Fifty Years of Social Progress, 1884-1934*. London: J. M. Dent and Sons, 1935.
Porter, John F., and William J. Wolf, eds. *Toward the Recovery of Unity*. New York: Seabury, 1964.

Ramsey, Arthur Michael. *F. D. Maurice and the Conflicts of Modern Theology*. Cambridge: Cambridge University Press, 1951.
Raven, Charles E. *Christian Socialism, 1848-1854*. London: Macmillan, 1920.
Reardon, Bernard M. G. *From Coleridge to Gore: A Century of Religious Thought in Britain*. London: Longmans, 1971.
Reckitt, Maurice B. *Maurice to Temple: A Century of the Social Movement in the Church of England*. London: Faber and Faber, 1947.
Reynolds, J. S. *The Evangelicals at Oxford, 1735-1871*. Oxford: Basil Blackwell, 1953.
Roberts, Michael J. D. "The Role of the Laity in the Church of England, c. 1850-1885." D.Phil. thesis, Oxford Univeristy, 1974.
Roberts, Ted. *Partners and Ministers*. London: Falcon Books, 1972.
Rose, Millicent. *The East End of London*. London: Cresset Press, 1951.
Russell, Anthony John. "A Sociological Analysis of the Clergyman's Role: With Special Reference to its Development in the Early Nineteenth Century." D.Phil. thesis, Oxford University, 1970.

Sanders, Charles Richard. *Coleridge and the Broad Church Movement*. Durham: Duke University Press, 1942.
Sinclair, Robert. *East London*. Vol. XXX of the *County Book Series*. London: Robert Hale, 1950.

Smith, Hubert Llewellyn. *The History of East London from the Earliest Times to the End of the Eighteenth Century*. London: Macmillan, 1939.

Smith, Warren Sylvester. *The London Heretics, 1870-1914*. London: Constable, 1967.

Stafford, Ann. *Light Me a Candle*. London: Hodder and Stoughton, 1949.

Stock, Eugene. *The History of the Church Missionary Society: Its Environment, Its Men, and Its Work*. 2 vols. London, 1899.

Thompson, David M. "The 1851 Religious Census: Problems and Possibilities." *Victorian Studies*, XI (1967), 87-97.

Thompson, E. P. *The Making of the English Working Class*. Harmondsworth: Penguin, 1969 [1963].

Thompson, Kenneth A. *Bureaucracy and Church Reform: The Organizational Response of the Church of England to Social Change, 1800-1965*. Oxford: Clarendon Press, 1970.

Wagner, Donald O. *The Church of England and Social Reform since 1854*. New York: privately printed, 1930.

Watkinson, Anthony R. K. "The Origins of Ritualism." Unpublished paper, 1968.

Wickham, E. R. *Church and People in an Industrial City*. London: Lutterworth Press, 1957.

Wyld, Peter. *Stepney Story: A Thousand Years of St. Dunstan's*. London: St. Catherine Press, 1952.

Young, Michael, and Peter Willmott. *Family and Kinship in East London*. Harmondsworth: Penguin, 1962 [1957].

Zabriskie, Alexander C., ed. *Anglican Evangelicalism*. Philadelphia: The Church Historical Society, 1943.